CREATIVE COOKING COLLECTION

Casseroles

CREATIVE COOKING COLLECTION

Casseroles
Mary Cadogan

CONTENTS

Published exclusively for Cupress (Canada) Limited
10 Falconer Drive, Unit 8, Mississauga,
Ontario L5N1B1, Canada
by Woodhead-Faulkner Ltd

First published 1988
© Woodhead-Faulkner (Publishers) Ltd 1988
ISBN 0-920691-29-3
Printed and bound in Italy by Arnoldo Mondadori Editore

INTRODUCTION

When you think of casseroles, does your mind go to school dinners? Then think again, because the casserole has changed its image! Look in this book and you will find colourful and tasty recipes, ranging from rich winter stews flavoured with aromatic herbs and cooked in wine or good stock, to light vegetable mixtures laced with garlic, tomatoes or yogurt. There are plenty of ideas, too, for the most special meal. Try Chinese Braised Lamb—gently cooked in ginger, soy sauce and cinnamon. In common with most of the recipes, it is simple to make and can be prepared well ahead of serving. Casseroles are never happier than when they are left to simmer slowly undisturbed, and need only some crusty bread or a simple vegetable to make the meal complete.

Every country has its own particular style. Locro is a favourite dish from South America where chick peas and kernel corn are cheap and plentiful. Cooked with beef in a rich tomato sauce it makes a satisfying meal. Osso Bucco is a favourite Italian stew made with knuckle of veal cooked in wine. A dusting of lemon peel and parsley gives it a beautifully fresh flavour. Saffron Seafood Casserole has a taste of France and a wonderful aroma.

The vegetarian chapter proves that meat is not needed to produce a hearty stew. Sauces enriched with plenty of vegetables, with a base of good stock, transform simple ingredients into delicious dishes. Spices, too, play an important role and add their warm fragrance to many meatless meals. Dhal Sambar is a gutsy combination of lentils, egg plants and tomatoes, well spiced with chillies and fresh coriander. For a more subtle taste, try Spinach and Zucchini Tian. If you are not a vegetarian, but in common with many of us are cutting down on meat to make your meals healthier, you will find many recipes to appeal to you.

Whatever your tastes, I have provided plenty of ideas for enjoyable meals for family, friends and special guests.

NOTES

Ingredients are given in both metric and imperial measures. Use either set of quantities but not a mixture of both in any one recipe.

All spoon measurements are level:
1 tablespoon = one 15 ml spoon
1 teaspoon = one 5 ml spoon.

Ovens should be preheated to the temperature specified.

Freshly ground black pepper is intended where pepper is listed.

Fresh herbs are used unless otherwise stated. If unobtainable dried herbs can be substituted in cooked dishes but halve the quantities.

Where a casserole should be 'covered tightly' and its lid does not fit snugly, place a piece of foil between the dish and lid to seal.

Basic stock recipes are marked with an asterisk and given in the reference section (pages 78–9).

OXTAIL CASSEROLE WITH ORANGE

Choose the thickest oxtail available for the best flavour and buy it ready cut into large pieces.

1 oxtail, weighing about
   1 kg (2 lb), cut into
   pieces
50 ml (¼ cup) flour
1 orange
2 tablespoons butter
1 tablespoon oil
2 onions, sliced
4 carrots, sliced
1 small turnip, chopped

450 ml (1¾ cups) Rich
   Beef Stock*
bouquet garni
1 tablespoon tomato paste
4 tablespoons port or
   sherry (optional)
salt and pepper to taste
2 tablespoons chopped
   parsley to garnish

Serves 4
Preparation time:
35 minutes
Cooking time:
2½–3 hours
Freezing:
Recommended

Illustrated top right: Boeuf en Daube (page 8)

1. Trim as much fat as possible from the oxtail. Season the flour with salt and pepper and use to coat the oxtail.
2. Peel the orange, taking care not to include the white pith. Set aside 2 pieces.
3. Cut the remaining peel into fine strips and blanch in boiling water for 5 minutes. Drain and set aside for garnish.
4. Squeeze the juice from the orange and set aside.
5. Heat the butter and oil in a large pan, add the oxtail and brown over a high heat, turning frequently. Transfer to a casserole dish.
6. Add the onion, carrot and turnip to the pan and fry until lightly browned. Gradually stir in the stock, then add the 2 reserved orange peel pieces, the orange juice, bouquet garni, tomato paste, port or sherry if using, and salt and pepper. Simmer for 5 minutes, stirring, then pour over the oxtail.
7. Cover the casserole tightly and cook in a preheated oven, 150°C/300°F, for 2½–3 hours, until the oxtail is tender.
8. Skim any surface fat from the casserole and discard the bouquet garni. Serve in wide soup plates, sprinkled with the reserved blanched orange strips and chopped parsley, with plenty of bread for mopping up the juices.

BOEUF EN DAUBE

A daube is similar to a pot roast in that the piece of meat is cooked in a flavoursome liquid—in this case a wine and tomato sauce, made more substantial with vegetables and kidney beans. A potato and carrot purée, sprinkled with chopped green onions, is a good accompaniment.

2 tablespoons oil	*2 cloves garlic, crushed*
1 kg (2 lb) piece topside or	*bouquet garni*
top rump beef	*398 ml (14 oz) can*
2 onions, chopped	*tomatoes*
3 carrots, chopped into	*300 ml (1¼ cups) red wine*
large chunks	*398 ml (14 oz) can red*
2 leeks, chopped into large	*kidney beans, drained*
chunks	*salt and pepper to taste*

Serves 4–6
Preparation time:
30 minutes
Cooking time:
2½ hours
Freezing:
Recommended

Illustrated on
page 7

1. Heat the oil in a flameproof casserole, add the beef and brown it all over. Remove the pan and set aside.
2. Add the onions, carrots, leeks and garlic to the casserole and fry gently for about 5 minutes, until well coated in oil and slightly softened.
3. Add the bouquet garni, tomatoes, wine, and salt and pepper and bring to the boil. Return the meat to the pan.
4. Cover tightly and cook in a preheated oven, 150°C/300°F, for 2 hours, until the meat is tender.
5. Stir in the kidney beans and return to the oven for 30 minutes.
6. To serve, remove the meat and slice it thinly. Discard the bouquet garni and any surface fat from the sauce, then serve it with the meat.

BEEF AND FENNEL POT ROAST

1.25 kg (2½ lb) piece	*1 tablespoon flour*
topside, or top rump beef	*2 tablespoons oil*
300 ml (1¼ cups) red wine	*½ teaspoon celery seeds*
1 teaspoon each chopped	*1 bulb fennel*
rosemary, thyme, bay	*2 teaspoons Dijon mustard*
and parsley	*150 ml (⅔ cup) Rich Beef*
1 onion, chopped finely	*Stock**
2 cloves garlic, crushed	*salt and pepper to taste*

1. Place the beef in a bowl, pour over the wine and add the herbs and onions. Cover and leave to marinate for at least 4 hours, or overnight, turning occasionally.

2. Remove the meat from the marinade and wipe it with paper towels; reserve the marinade. Rub the garlic over the meat and sprinkle with the flour, and salt and pepper.

3. Heat the oil in a flameproof casserole, add the beef and fry on all sides until evenly browned. Drain off excess oil. Add the reserved marinade, celery seeds and salt and pepper and bring to the boil. Cover tightly and cook in a preheated oven, 150°C/300°F, for 1½ hours.

4. Remove the leaves from the fennel and set aside. Cut the bulb into 8 wedges and add to the casserole. Return to the oven for 1 hour, until the meat is tender.

5. Transfer the meat and fennel to a warmed serving dish and keep warm.

6. Strain the cooking juices into a small pan and skim off the fat from the surface. Add the mustard and stock, bring to the boil, then simmer for 5 minutes. Check the seasoning and adjust if necessary.

7. Pour a little sauce over the meat and fennel and garnish with the reserved fennel leaves. Serve the remaining sauce separately. Serve with broccoli with almonds, and creamed potatoes topped with oatmeal and grated cheese, then browned under a broiler.

Serves 6–8
Preparation time: 20 minutes, plus marinating
Cooking time: 2½ hours
Freezing: Recommended

Illustrated above: Beef and Fennel Pot Roast

SPICED BEEF WITH BEANS

2 tablespoons oil
1.25 kg (2½ lb) braising
    steak, cubed
2 onions, chopped
2 cloves garlic, crushed
1 teaspoon chilli powder
2 teaspoons ground cumin
1 teaspoon chopped
    marjoram
4 tablespoons tomato
    paste

2 bay leaves
450 ml (1¾ cups) Rich
    Beef Stock*
1 each red and yellow
    pepper, cored, seeded
    and chopped
398 ml (14 oz) can red
    kidney beans, drained
250 ml (1 cup) thick
    yogurt
salt and pepper to taste

Serves 6–8
Preparation time:
25 minutes
Cooking time:
1 hour 50 minutes
Freezing:
Recommended, at
end of stage 3

1. Heat the oil in a large pan, add the beef and fry until lightly browned. Add the onions and garlic and cook for 5 minutes. Stir in the chilli, cumin and marjoram and cook for 1 minute.
2. Add the tomato paste, bay leaves, stock, and salt and pepper, bring to the boil, then cover and simmer for 1½ hours, until the beef is tender.
3. Stir in the peppers and beans and cook for 15 minutes.
4. Gradually stir in the yogurt and simmer for 5 minutes. Discard the bay leaves. Serve with rice mixed with grains.

BEEF IN BEER WITH MUSTARD SEED DUMPLINGS

You will need a wide casserole dish which will hold all the dumplings, or cook the stew in two pots.

2 tablespoons oil
1.25 kg (2½ lb) stewing
    beef, cubed
2 onions, sliced thinly
3 celery sticks, chopped
3 carrots, sliced
50 ml (¼ cup) flour
450 ml (1¾ cups) beer
150 ml (⅔ cup) Rich Beef
    Stock*
2 teaspoons light brown
    sugar

2 bay leaves
2 teaspoons Worcestershire
    sauce
1 tablespoon tomato paste
salt and pepper to taste
FOR THE DUMPLINGS:
250 ml (1 cup) self-raising
    flour, sifted
2 teaspoons mustard seeds
50 g (2 oz) shredded suet
½ teaspoon salt
2–3 tablespoons water

1. Heat the oil in a large pan, add the beef and fry until browned. Transfer the meat to a large casserole dish.

2. Add the vegetables to the pan and fry for 5 minutes. Stir in the flour and cook for 1 minute. Gradually stir in the beer and stock, cooking until thickened.

3. Add the remaining ingredients, pour over the beef and stir well. Cover the casserole and cook in a preheated oven, 170°C/325°F, for about 2 hours, until the meat is tender.

4. Meanwhile, make the dumplings. Mix together the flour, mustard seeds, suet and salt. Add enough water to mix to a soft dough. Shape into 16 balls and place on top of the casserole, cover and return to the oven for 20–25 minutes, until the dumplings are risen and light. Discard the bay leaves.

5. Serve with boiled new potatoes in their skins, sprinkled with parsley.

Serves 6–8
Preparation time
40 minutes
Cooking time:
About 2½ hours
Freezing:
Recommended, at end of stage 3

LAMB AND KIDNEY HOTPOT

1 tablespoon flour	1 tablespoon
750 g (1½ lb) boneless	Worcestershire sauce
lamb, cut into 2.5 cm	1 teaspoon chopped
(1 inch) cubes	rosemary
4 lambs' kidneys, cored	300 ml (1¼ cups) Light
and quartered	Meat Stock*
1 tablespoon oil	750 g (1½ lb) potatoes in
2 onions, chopped	their skins, sliced
2 carrots, sliced	1 tablespoon butter
1 tablespoon tomato paste	salt and pepper to taste
	rosemary sprigs to garnish

Serves 4–6
Preparation time:
35 minutes
Cooking timeL
1–1¼ hours
Freezing:
Not recommended

1. Season the flour with salt and pepper and use to coat the lamb and kidneys.
2. Heat the oil in a large pan, add the onion and carrot and cook until softened. Add the lamb and kidneys and fry until browned. Stir in tomato paste, Worcestershire sauce, rosemary, stock, and salt and pepper, and bring to the boil.
3. Arrange half of the potato over the base of a casserole dish. Place the meat mixture on top and cover with the remaining potato. Dot with the butter.
4. Cook, uncovered, in a preheated oven, 150°C/300°F, for 1–1¼ hours, until the potato is browned. Serve garnished with rosemary.

MINTY LAMB WITH PINE NUTS

2 tablespoons oil	75 g (3 oz) dried apricots,
1 large onion, chopped	chopped
1 kg (2 lb) boneless lamb,	3 tablespoons chopped
cubed	mint
450 ml (1¾ cups) Light	50 g (2 oz) pine nuts
Meat Stock*	salt and pepper to taste
1 tablespoon wine vinegar	mint sprigs to garnish
1 tablespoon liquid honey	

Serves 6
Preparation time:
25 minutes
Cooking time:
1¼ hours
Freezing:
Recommended

1. Heat the oil in a large pan, add the onion and fry until lightly browned. Add the lamb and stir well.
2. Add the stock, vinegar, honey and apricots. Bring to the boil, then cover and simmer for 1 hour, stirring occasionally.
3. Add the mint, pine nuts, and salt and pepper and simmer for 15 minutes. Garnish with mint and serve with saffron rice.

LAMB AND ALE STEW WITH PAPRIKA BREAD

Use real ale if possible as it gives the best flavour.

1 tablespoon flour
1 kg (2 lb) lamb fillet, cut
   into 2.5 cm (1 inch)
   cubes
1 tablespoon oil
2 onions, chopped
3 carrots, sliced
2 celery sticks, sliced
300 ml (1¼ cups) beer
1 teaspoon Dijon mustard

1 teaspoon Worcestershire
   sauce
2 teaspoons sugar
salt and pepper to taste
FOR THE TOPPING:
2 large slices white bread,
   crusts removed
2 tablespoons butter
1 teaspoon paprika

Serves 6
Preparation time:
20 minutes
Cooking time:
1½ hours
Freezing:
Recommended, at
end of stage 3

1. Season the flour with salt and pepper and use to coat the lamb.
2. Heat the oil in a flameproof casserole, add the onion and fry until lightly browned. Add the lamb and remaining ingredients, bring to the boil, then simmer for 5 minutes.
3. Cover the casserole tightly and cook in a preheated oven, 180°C/350°F, for 1 hour.
4. Meanwhile, cut each slice of bread into 16 pieces.
5. Place the butter and paprika in a pan and heat gently until melted. Brush this mixture over one side of each piece of bread.
6. Cover the casserole with the bread, buttered side up and overlapping the pieces. Return to the oven, uncovered, for 30 minutes, until the bread topping is crisp and brown at the edges. Serve with leeks or green beans.

BOSTON BEAN POT

500 g (1 lb) dried white
   beans, soaked overnight
2 onions, chopped
2 celery sticks, chopped
2 tablespoons Dijon
   mustard
2 tablespoons light brown
   sugar

3 tablespoons molasses
2 tablespoons wine
   vinegar
pinch of ground cloves
1 tablespoon tomato paste
750 g (1½ lb) piece side
   pork
½ teaspoon salt (optional)

1. Drain the beans and cook in boiling water for 10 minutes. Drain, then place in a flameproof casserole with the onion and celery.

2. Mix together the mustard, sugar, molasses, vinegar, cloves and tomato paste, add to the pan and top up with water until the beans are just covered.

3. Bury the pork in the beans. Bring the mixture slowly to the boil, skimming off any scum. Stir the beans.

4. Cover the casserole tightly and cook in a preheated oven, 180°C/350°F, for 2–2½ hours, until the beans are very tender; add a little boiling water halfway through the cooking if the mixture seems dry. Add the salt if using, and stir well.

5. To serve, remove the pork from the pot and cut into large chunks or slices, then return to the beans. Serve with whole wheat rolls.

Serves 6
Preparation time:
15 minutes, plus
soaking time
Cooking time:
2–2½ hours
Freezing:
Recommended

PORK MEATBALLS IN RED WINE

Make this dish the day before you need it, if you wish—it reheats well and I think the taste is even improved.

125 ml (½ cup) whole
   wheat breadcrumbs
2 onions, grated or
   chopped finely
1 kg (2 lb) ground pork
1 tablespoon mixed
   chopped herbs, e.g. sage,
   thyme, rosemary,
   marjoram

2 tablespoons oil
398 ml (14 oz) can
   tomatoes
300 ml (1¼ cups) red
   wine
250 g (8 oz) button
   mushrooms, sliced
1 teaspoon sugar
salt and pepper to taste

Serves 6–8
Preparation time:
40 minutes
Cooking time:
30 minutes
Freezing:
Recommended

1. Mix together the breadcrumbs, onion, pork, herbs, and salt and pepper, and shape into 24 balls with wetted hands.
2. Heat the oil in a frying pan, add the meatballs in batches and fry until evenly browned. Drain on paper towels.
3. Place the tomatoes, wine, mushrooms, sugar, and salt and pepper in a large pan and stir well to mix. Bring to the boil, add the meatballs and stir until they are all coated in the sauce. Cover and simmer for 30 minutes, until tender.
4. Serve the meatballs with green noodles or brown rice and a crisp leafy salad.

PORK WITH MUNG BEANS

Mung beans are tiny little green dried beans most often used for sprouting. They do not require soaking.

350 g (12 oz) mung beans
2 bay leaves
2 onions
2 cloves
450 ml (1¾ cups) Chicken or Vegetable Stock*
2 carrots, sliced
2 celery sticks, sliced
2 tablespoons chopped celery leaves
125 g (4 oz) mushrooms, sliced
4 pork shoulder chops
1 teaspoon chopped marjoram
salt and pepper to taste

1. Place the beans in a pan with water to cover. Add the bay leaves and one onion stuck with the cloves. Bring to the boil, then cover and simmer for 40–45 minutes, until the beans are fairly tender. Drain, then discard the bay leaves and onion. Return the beans to the pan.
2. Chop the remaining onion and add to the pan with the stock, carrot, celery, celery leaves and mushrooms. Mix well and season with salt and pepper.
3. Sprinkle the pork with the marjoram and push into the beans. Bring to the boil, then cover and simmer for 35–40 minutes, until tender. Serve with whole wheat bread.

Serves 4
Preparation time: 20 minutes
Cooking time: 1¼–1½ hours
Freezing: Recommended

PORK AND RED CABBAGE BAKE

Red cabbage cooked with apples and wine vinegar is a delicious foil for rich pork. A crunchy potato topping completes the dish. Serve it with crusty bread.

2 tablespoons oil
500 g (1 lb) pork shoulder
or tenderloin, cubed
1 teaspoon cumin seeds
1 onion, chopped finely
750 g (1½ lb) red cabbage,
shredded
1 cooking apple, peeled,
cored and chopped

1 tablespoon light brown
sugar
1 tablespoon wine vinegar
50 ml (¼ cup) raisins
150 ml (⅔ cup) Chicken
Stock*
750 g (1½ lb) potatoes,
par-boiled in their skins
and cubed
salt and pepper to taste

Serves 4
Preparation time:
35 minutes
Cooking time:
45–50 minutes
Freezing:
Recommended

1. Heat half of the oil in a large pan, add the pork and fry until lightly browned. Remove and set aside.
2. Add the cumin seeds and onion to the pan and fry for about 2 minutes, stirring. Add the cabbage, apple, sugar, vinegar, raisins, stock, and salt and pepper. Bring to the boil, then simmer for 3–4 minutes, until the cabbage has softened slightly.
3. Toss the potatoes in the remaining oil, and sprinkle with salt and pepper. Place half of the cabbage mixture in an ovenproof dish and spoon over the pork. Cover with the remaining cabbage, then top with the potatoes.
4. Cook in a preheated oven, 180°C/350°F, for 45–50 minutes, until the topping is crisp and golden.

RABBIT WITH PRUNES AND WALNUTS

Prunes, walnuts and a dash of wine make this simple rabbit dish classy enough to serve to guests.

1 tablespoon flour
500 g (1 lb) diced boneless
rabbit
1 tablespoon oil
2 tablespoons butter
175 g (6 oz) side bacon,
chopped
125 g (4 oz) pickling
onions
3 celery sticks, chopped

1 bay leaf
1 blade mace
12 ready-to-eat prunes
150 ml (⅔ cup) white wine
300 ml (1¼ cups) Chicken
Stock*
50 g (2 oz) walnut pieces
3 tablespoons table cream
salt and pepper to taste

1. Season the flour with salt and pepper and use to coat the rabbit.
2. Heat the oil and butter in a large saucepan or flame-proof casserole, add the rabbit and fry until evenly browned. Remove from the pan and set aside.
3. Add the bacon and onions to the pan and fry until lightly coloured. Add the celery, bay leaf, mace, prunes, wine and stock, bring to the boil, then simmer for 5 minutes, stirring. Return the rabbit to the pan with the walnuts, and salt and pepper, cover and simmer for 35–40 minutes, until the rabbit is tender. Discard the bay leaf and mace.
4. Transfer the rabbit, bacon, onions, prunes and walnuts to a warmed serving dish with a slotted spoon. Keep warm.
5. Boil the sauce rapidly until reduced by a third. Check the seasoning and stir in the cream. Pour over the rabbit.
6. Serve with steamed potatoes, green beans sprinkled with sesame seeds, and a mixed salad.

Serves 6
Preparation time:
20 minutes
Cooking time:
35–40 minutes
Freezing:
Recommended

CHICKEN STOVIES WITH PARSLEY

Always use old potatoes for this dish as new ones do not cook well this way.

1 tablespoon oil	*125 g (4 oz) mushrooms,*
125 g (4 oz) side bacon,	*sliced*
chopped	*3 tablespoons chopped*
2 onions, sliced	*parsley*
1 kg (2 lb) potatoes, sliced	*300 ml (1¼ cups) Chicken*
thinly	*Stock**
350 g (12 oz) boneless	*salt and pepper to taste*
chicken breast, cubed	*parsley sprigs to garnish*

Serves 4
Preparation time:
30 minutes
Cooking time:
1 hour
Freezing:
Not recommended

1. Heat the oil in a large frying pan, add the bacon and fry until it is slightly crispy. Add the onions and fry until softened. Remove from the heat.
2. Arrange half of the sliced potato in a greased 1.5 litre (6 cup) shallow ovenproof dish and cover with the bacon and onion mixture. Arrange the chicken and mushrooms on top and sprinkle with the parsley, and salt and pepper.
3. Cover the chicken with the remaining potato. Pour over the stock and sprinkle with salt and pepper.
4. Cook, uncovered, in a preheated oven, 190°C/375°F, for 1 hour, until the potatoes are cooked and the top is golden brown. Serve garnished with parsley.

CHICKEN AND TARRAGON BRAISE

1 large lemon	*4 teaspoons chopped*
1 chicken with giblets,	*tarragon*
weighing 1.5 kg (3½ lb)	*1 bay leaf*
2 tablespoons butter	*300 ml (1¼ cups) water*
1 tablespoon oil	*2 tablespoons table cream*
1 onion, chopped	*or yogurt*
3 carrots, chopped	*salt and pepper to taste*
2 celery sticks, chopped	*tarragon sprigs to garnish*

1. Halve the lemon, cut a few slices from each half and set aside for garnish, then squeeze the juice. Rinse the chicken giblets and set aside. Place the squeezed lemon halves inside the chicken.
2. Heat the butter and oil in a saucepan or flameproof casserole large enough to hold the chicken snugly. Add the chicken and fry for about 10 minutes, until evenly browned all over. Remove and set aside.

3. Add the vegetables to the pan and fry for 5 minutes. Add the giblets, lemon juice, half of the tarragon, bay leaf, water, and salt and pepper. Bring to the boil, return the chicken to the pan, cover and simmer for 1¼–1½ hours.
4. Remove the chicken, place on a warmed serving dish and keep warm. Discard the giblets and bay leaf.
5. Purée the vegetable mixture in a food processor or blender; add a little stock or milk if the sauce is too thick. Return to the pan and stir in the cream or yogurt and reserved tarragon. Reheat gently and check the seasoning.
6. Garnish the chicken with the reserved lemon slices and tarragon, and serve with the sauce. Serve green beans, cooked with tomatoes and garlic, and sauté potatoes as accompaniments.

Serves 4–5
Preparation time:
40 minutes
Cooking time:
1½–1¾ hours
Freezing:
Not recommended

CHICKEN AND CORN CASSEROLE

1 tablespoon paprika
1 tablespoon flour
4 chicken portions, halved
2 tablespoons oil
1 onion, chopped
398 ml (14 oz) can
* tomatoes*
2 teaspoons Worcestershire
* sauce*

2 teaspoons made mustard
1 tablespoon light brown
* sugar*
2 tablespoons wine vinegar
1 red pepper, cored, seeded
* and cut into strips*
250 ml (1 cup) frozen
* kernel corn*
salt and pepper to taste

Serves 4
Preparation time:
25 minutes
Cooking time:
35–40 minutes
Freezing:
Recommended

1. Mix together the paprika, flour, and salt and pepper and use to coat the chicken pieces.
2. Heat the oil in a saucepan, add half of the chicken pieces and fry until browned; remove. Fry the remaining pieces; remove. Drain off most of the oil.
3. Add the onion to the pan and fry until softened. Add the tomatoes, Worcestershire sauce, mustard, sugar and vinegar and bring to the boil, stirring constantly.
4. Return the chicken to the pan, cover and simmer for 35–40 minutes, until tender. Add the red pepper and kernel corn after 20 minutes.
5. Serve with baked potatoes.

FRANKFURTER AND BACON CASSEROLE

125 g (4 oz) bacon, halved
1 tablespoon oil
1 onion, chopped
1 each red and green
* pepper, cored, seeded*
* and chopped*
6 frankfurters (weiners),
* sliced*

150 ml (²/₃ cup) Rich
* Vegetable Stock**
2 teaspoons corn starch,
* blended with 150 ml*
* (²/₃ cup) milk*
175 g (6 oz) frozen kernel
* corn*
salt and pepper to taste

Serves 4
Preparation time:
25 minutes
Cooking time:
25–30 minutes
Freezing:
Not recommended

1. Stretch the bacon pieces on a board with the back of a knife, then roll up tightly.
2. Heat the oil in a saucepan, add the bacon rolls and fry quickly until lightly browned. Remove and set aside. Add the onion and pepper to the pan and fry for 5 minutes.
3. Add the frankfurters, bacon rolls and stock, bring to the boil, then cover and simmer for 15–20 minutes.
4. Stir in the blended corn starch and kernel corn and simmer for 10 minutes. Check seasoning. Serve with brown rice, flavoured with herbs.

BACON AND BEAN STEW

I recently discovered these excellent light dumplings
flavoured with garlic and chives.

250 g (8 oz) dried white
   beans, soaked overnight
900 ml (3²/₃ cups) water
500 g (1 lb) piece salt pork,
   derinded and cubed
2 onions, chopped
250 g (8 oz) carrots, cut
   into large pieces
4 celery sticks, cut into
   large pieces
2 cloves garlic, crushed
250 g (8 oz) tomatoes,
   skinned and chopped

2 bay leaves
3 thyme sprigs
snipped chives to garnish
FOR THE DUMPLINGS:
250 ml (1 cup) self-raising
   flour, sifted
1 tablespoon snipped
   chives
1 teaspoon salt
1 clove garlic, crushed
50 ml (¹/₄ cup) shortening
4–5 tablespoons water
pepper to taste

Serves 4–6
Preparation time:
25 minutes, plus
soaking time
Cooking time:
1½–1¾ hours
Freezing:
Not recommended

1. Drain the beans and cook in boiling water for 10
minutes, then drain and place in a large saucepan with the
remaining ingredients. Bring slowly to the boil, skimming
off any scum, then cover and simmer for 1–1¼ hours, until
the bacon is tender, skimming occasionally.
2. Meanwhile, make the dumplings. Mix together the
flour, chives, salt, garlic, shortening and pepper. Add the
water, mix to a soft dough and knead briefly. Using lightly
floured hands, shape the mixture into 8 balls.
3. Drop the dumplings into the stew, cover tightly and
simmer for 25 minutes, until they are light and puffy.
4. Serve in soup plates, sprinkled with snipped chives.

SAUSAGE AND POTATO CASSEROLE

This is a great favourite in our family and it couldn't be
more simple. Hot American or spicy Italian sausages have
the best flavour.

2 tablespoons oil
2 large onions, sliced
   thinly
1 kg (2 lb) spicy sausages,
   skinned and quartered
1.5 kg (3 lb) potatoes,
   sliced thinly

450 ml (1³/₄ cups) Rich
   Vegetable Stock*
175 g (6 oz) old Cheddar
   cheese, grated
4 tablespoons chopped
   parsley
salt and pepper to taste

1. Heat the oil in a large pan, add the onion and fry gently until lightly browned.

2. Increase the heat, add the sausages and brown quickly. Remove from the heat.

3. Place half of the potatoes in a large buttered gratin dish, sprinkling each layer with salt and pepper. Cover with the sausage mixture, then top with the remaining potatoes, seasoning each layer. Pour in the stock.

4. Cook, uncovered, in a preheated oven, 190°C/375°F, for 1 hour, until the potatoes are tender.

5. Sprinkle with the cheese and parsley and return to the oven for 15 minutes. Serve with a green salad.

Serves 6–8
Preparation time:
30 minutes
Cooking time:
1¼ hours
Freezing:
Not recommended

INDIAN FISHBALL CURRY

Sweet-tasting coconut tastes remarkably good in this fish dish, particularly combined with subtle spices. Serve the curry with saffron rice and traditional accompaniments. A tomato salad, topped with yogurt and paprika, goes well.

750 g (1½ lb) cod fillet	2 green chillies, seeded and
150 ml (⅔ cup) each milk	chopped finely
and water	3 tablespoons oil
150 ml (⅔ cup) desiccated	2 teaspoons each garam
coconut	masala, ground
300 ml (1¼ cups) boiling	coriander and cumin
water	1 teaspoon turmeric
1 egg, beaten	3 tablespoons lemon juice
1 onion, grated	2 teaspoons tomato paste
2 potatoes, boiled and	salt to taste
mashed	mint sprigs to garnish

Serves 4
Preparation time:
40 minutes
Cooking time:
About 30 minutes
Freezing:
Recommended

1. Place the cod in a shallow pan and add the milk and water. Bring to the boil, then cover and simmer for 10–12 minutes, until the fish flakes easily. Drain and flake the fish, discarding the skin and any bones.
2. Place the coconut in a bowl and pour over the boiling water. Leave to infuse for 20 minutes, then strain through a sieve, pressing out as much liquid as possible, and set aside. Reserve the coconut.
3. Mix the flaked fish in a bowl with the egg, onion, potato, chillies and salt. Form into 12–14 balls.
4. Heat the oil in a large frying pan, add the fishballs and fry carefully on all sides until lightly browned, then remove with a slotted spoon and drain on paper towels.
5. Add the spices to the pan and cook for 1 minute, stirring well. Add the lemon juice, coconut liquid and tomato paste and bring to the boil. Add 1 tablespoon of the reserved coconut and a little salt and simmer for 10 minutes, stirring occasionally.
6. Add the fishballs to the sauce, cover and simmer for 10 minutes, turning after 5 minutes.
7. Toast 1 tablespoon of the reserved coconut under a preheated broiler until lightly browned. Serve the fishballs in the sauce, sprinkled with the toasted coconut and garnished with mint.

SOUTH AMERICAN BEEF POT

It's always useful to find another recipe for using ground
beef, and this one is particularly tasty.

750 g (1 1/2 lb) ground beef	*1 large green pepper,*
2 beef bouillon cubes,	*cored, seeded and*
crumbled	*chopped*
1 tablespoon flour	*4 tablespoons chopped*
1 kg (2 lb) potatoes, sliced	*parsley*
thinly	*3 eggs*
550 g (1.2 lb) jar passata	*150 ml (2/3 cup) milk*
1 Spanish onion, chopped	*salt and pepper to taste*

Serves 4–6
Preparation time:
30 minutes
Cooking time:
1 1/4 hours
Freezing:
Not recommended

1. Place the beef in a flameproof casserole or heavy-based
saucepan and heat gently, stirring, for about 15 minutes,
until the fat runs and the grains are separate.
2. Sprinkle over the beef bouillon cubes and flour and
cook for 1 minute. Remove half of the beef and set aside.
3. Cover the beef in the pan with half of the potato, then
top with half each of the passata, onion, green pepper and
parsley, seasoning each layer well with salt and pepper.
Cover with the remaining beef and repeat the layers,
reserving a little parsley and chopped pepper for garnish.
4. Cover the pan and cook gently for 1 hour, until the
potatoes are cooked and the beef is tender.
5. Beat the eggs with the milk, and salt and pepper, pour
over the casserole, cover and cook gently for 10–15
minutes, until the egg mixture is set. Sprinkle with the
reserved parsley and pepper to serve.

RED-COOKED BEEF

Any leftover meat can be reheated in the cooking liquid
with more vegetables or noodles the next day.

1.25–1.5 kg (2 1/2–3 lb)	*2 pieces star anise*
shank of beef, in one	*2 teaspoons sesame oil*
piece	*(optional)*
300 ml (1 1/4 cups) soy	*250 g (8 oz) beansprouts*
sauce	*1 small head Chinese*
3 tablespoons dry sherry	*cabbage, sliced thinly*
5 slices fresh ginger root	*500 g (1 lb) spinach,*
2 cloves garlic, bruised	*shredded*
300 ml (1 1/4 cups) water	*shredded green onion to*
2 teaspoons liquid honey	*garnish*

1. Tie the beef into a neat shape and place in a pan slightly bigger than the meat. Add the soy sauce, sherry, ginger, garlic, water, honey, star anise and sesame oil, if using. Bring to the boil, then cover and simmer for 2½–3 hours, until the meat is very tender; turn several times during cooking.

2. Remove the meat from the liquid and leave to cool for 10 minutes. Cut into the thinnest possible slices and keep warm. Remove the ginger, garlic and star anise from the liquid with a slotted spoon. Bring the liquid to the boil.

3. Mix together the beansprouts, Chinese cabbage and spinach. Plunge half of the vegetables into the pan and cook for 2 minutes. Remove with a slotted spoon and arrange on a warmed serving dish. Keep warm. Repeat with the remaining vegetables.

4. Arrange the meat on the vegetables. Pour a little of the cooking liquid over the top and sprinkle the green onions over the meat.

Serves 6–8
Preparation time: 20 minutes
Cooking time: 2½–3 hours
Freezing: Recommended, at end of stage 1

CREOLE BEEF CASSEROLE

This colourful casserole from Louisiana is traditionally cooked in a hollowed-out pumpkin.

2 tablespoons oil
1 Spanish onion, chopped
2 cloves garlic, crushed
1 kg (2 lb) stewing beef, cubed
398 ml (14 oz) can tomatoes
600 ml (2½ cups) Rich Beef Stock*
2 teaspoons chopped marjoram

1 bay leaf
1 sweet potato, sliced
500 g (1 lb) pumpkin, cubed
3 potatoes, cubed
398 ml (14 oz) can baby corn cobs, drained
398 ml (14 oz) can peach halves in syrup
salt and pepper to taste
marjoram sprigs to garnish

Serves 6–8
Preparation time: 35 minutes
Cooking time: 2¾ hours
Freezing: Recommended

1. Heat the oil in a large saucepan or flameproof casserole, add the onion and garlic and fry gently until softened. Add the beef and cook, stirring, until browned all over. Add the tomatoes, stock, marjoram and bay leaf. Bring to the boil, then cover and simmer for 2 hours.
2. Add the sweet potato, pumpkin, potato and corn cobs. Drain the peaches and add the syrup, and salt and pepper. Simmer for 30 minutes, until the vegetables are tender.
3. Stir in the peach halves and cook for 10 minutes. Serve garnished with marjoram sprigs.

LOCRO

This dish is popular in South America. If you can't get chorizo sausage, use cabanos instead.

2 tablespoons oil
2 large onions, sliced
750 g (1½ lb) stewing beef, cubed
398 ml (14 oz) can tomatoes
150 ml (⅔ cup) water
2 tablespoons paprika
½ teaspoon cayenne pepper

398 ml (14 oz) can chick peas, drained
125 g (4 oz) chorizo sausage, sliced
250 ml (1 cup) frozen kernel corn
salt to taste
50 g (2 oz) Mozzarella cheese, chopped, to serve

1. Heat the oil in a large saucepan, add the onion and fry until softened and lightly coloured. Add the meat and fry, stirring, for 5 minutes.

2. Stir in the tomatoes with their juice, water, paprika, cayenne and salt. Bring to the boil, then cover and simmer for 1¾–2 hours, until the meat is almost tender.

3. Stir in the chick peas, chorizo and kernel corn and simmer for 30 minutes.

4. Transfer to a warmed serving dish or individual soup plates and sprinkle with pieces of Mozzarella cheese.

Serves 6
Preparation time: 35 minutes
Cooking time: 2¼–2½ hours
Freezing: Recommended, at end of stage 3

KOFTA CURRY

1 kg (2 lb) lamb or beef	2 teaspoons each ground
2 onions, 1 grated and 1	coriander and cumin
chopped	1 teaspoon turmeric
2.5 cm (1 inch) piece fresh	1 cinnamon stick
ginger root, peeled and	4 cloves
grated	450 ml (1³/₄ cups) water
2 cloves garlic, crushed	1 tablespoon tomato paste
2 green chillies, seeded and	125 ml (¹/₂ cup) raisins
chopped finely	125 ml (¹/₂ cup) blanched
3 tablespoons chopped	almonds
coriander leaves	300 ml (1¹/₄ cups) thick
1 egg, beaten	yogurt
2 tablespoons oil	salt and pepper to taste

Serves 6–8
Preparation time:
30 minutes
Cooking time:
30 minutes
Freezing:
Recommended, at
end of stage 4

1. Place the meat, grated onion, ginger, garlic, chillies, chopped coriander, egg, and salt and pepper in a bowl and mix with the hands or a fork until thoroughly combined. Shape into 40 small balls with wetted hands.
2. Heat the oil in a large pan, add the meatballs in batches and fry for about 5 minutes, until evenly browned. Remove with a slotted spoon and drain well on paper towels.
3. Drain off excess oil from the pan. Add the chopped onion to the pan and fry until lightly browned. Stir in the ground coriander, cumin and turmeric. Add the cinnamon stick and cloves and cook for 1 minute. Stir in the water, tomato paste and raisins and bring to the boil.
4. Return the meatballs to the pan and stir well. Cover and simmer for 30 minutes, until tender. Stir in the almonds.
5. Stir in the yogurt a tablespoon at a time. Check the seasoning. Serve with turmeric flavoured rice.

MIDDLE EASTERN LAMB MEATBALLS

2 slices white bread, crusts	2 tablespoons oil
removed	50 g (2 oz) pine nuts
50 g (2 oz) seedless raisins	4 tablespoons lemon juice
1 kg (2 lb) ground lamb	300 ml (1¹/₄ cups) water
2 onions, grated or	600 ml (2¹/₂ cups) thick
chopped finely	yogurt
2 teaspoons ground cumin	4 tablespoons corn starch
1 tablespoon ground	2 tablespoons chopped
coriander	parsley
	salt and pepper to taste

1. Soak the bread in water to cover for 5 minutes, then squeeze well and crumble into a bowl.

2. Coarsely chop the raisins. Add to the bowl with the lamb, onion, cumin, coriander, and salt and pepper. Squeeze the mixture with your fingers until evenly mixed. Shape into about 32 small meatballs with wetted hands.

3. Heat the oil in a large pan and fry the meatballs in batches for about 5 minutes, until evenly browned. Drain off any excess fat from the pan.

4. Return the meatballs to the pan and add the pine nuts, lemon juice, water, and salt and pepper. Bring to the boil, then cover and simmer for 20 minutes.

5. Blend the yogurt with the corn starch and gradually stir into the pan. Bring to a gentle simmer and cook for about 5 minutes, until heated through. Stir in the parsley.

6. Serve with rice mixed with lightly fried grated carrot and cumin seeds.

Serves 6–8
Preparation time:
40 minutes
Cooking time:
30 minutes
Freezing:
Not recommended

LAMB AND LENTIL CURRY

2 tablespoons oil
2 onions, sliced thinly
1 clove garlic, crushed
2.5 cm (1 inch) piece fresh
  ginger root, peeled and
  grated
2 teaspoons cumin seeds
500 g (1 lb) boneless lamb,
  e.g. leg or fillet, cubed
250 g (8 oz) tomatoes,
  skinned and chopped

1 teaspoon each ground
  cumin, coriander and
  turmeric
1/2 teaspoon chilli powder
600 ml (2 1/2 cups) water
250 g (8 oz) red lentils
2 tablespoons lemon juice
1 teaspoon garam masala
salt to taste

Serves 4
Preparation time:
30 minutes
Cooking time:
1 hour
Freezing:
Recommended, at
end of stage 3

1. Heat 1 tablespoon of the oil in a saucepan, add the onion, garlic, ginger and half of the cumin seeds and fry until the onion is softened and lightly browned. Add the lamb and cook, stirring, until well browned.
2. Add the tomatoes, cumin, coriander, turmeric, chilli powder and salt and stir well. Add the water and bring to the boil, then cover and simmer for 30 minutes.
3. Add the lentils and cook for 30 minutes or until the lamb and lentils are tender.
4. Just before serving, stir in the lemon juice and garam masala. Transfer to a warmed serving dish and keep warm.
5. Heat the remaining oil in a pan, add the remaining cumin seeds and fry quickly until they start to spit. Pour over the curry. Serve with rice and curry accompaniments.

LAMB MUGLAI

If you bone the lamb yourself, allow about 500 g (1 lb) of the total weight for the bone when buying the meat.

1.25–1.5 kg (2 1/2–3 lb)
  boneless lamb, cut into
  2.5 cm (1 inch) cubes
600 ml (2 1/2 cups) water
5 cm (2 inch) piece
  cinnamon stick
2 bay leaves
8 cloves
6 cardamom pods
2 tablespoons oil
2 onions, chopped
1 tablespoon curry powder

2 teaspoons ground
  coriander
2 teaspoons garam masala
1/2 teaspoon hot chilli
  powder
5 tablespoons tomato paste
750 g (1 1/2 lb) potatoes, cut
  into 2.5 cm (1 inch)
  chunks
500 ml (2 cups) thick
  yogurt

1. Place the lamb in a saucepan with the water, cinnamon stick, bay leaves, cloves and cardamom pods. Bring to the boil, then cover and simmer for 30 minutes.

2. Remove the meat with a slotted spoon and set aside. Strain the liquid into a jug.

3. Heat the oil in a saucepan, add the onion and fry gently until softened and lightly browned.

4. Add the lamb and the strained liquid, the spices, tomato paste and potatoes. Bring to the boil, stirring well, then cover and simmer for 25–30 minutes, until the lamb is very tender and the potatoes are cooked.

5. Stir in the yogurt a tablespoon at a time, stirring well and heating after each addition; do not allow to boil.

6. Serve the muglai with saffron rice, warm pitta bread and a shredded lettuce, cucumber and onion salad.

Serves 6–8
Preparation time:
20 minutes
Cooking time:
1 hour
Freezing:
Recommended, at
end of stage 4

CORIANDER CURRIED CHICKEN

125 ml (¹/₂ cup) desiccated
   coconut
150 ml (²/₃ cup) boiling
   water
2 teaspoons turmeric
4 chicken quarters, halved
2 tablespoons oil
1 onion, sliced
1 tablespoon crunchy
   peanut butter

¹/₂ teaspoon fennel seeds
¹/₂ teaspoon cumin seeds
¹/₂ teaspoon ground
   coriander
¹/₂ teaspoon black pepper
2 green chillies, chopped
   finely
strip of lemon peel
1 tablespoon lemon juice
coriander leaves to garnish

Serves 4
Preparation time:
40 minutes, plus
standing time
Cooking time:
35–40 minutes
Freezing:
Recommended

1. Soak the coconut in the boiling water for 20 minutes, then strain and set aside the liquid; discard the coconut.
2. Rub the turmeric into the chicken pieces.
3. Heat the oil in a large saucepan, add the onion and fry until lightly browned. Stir in the peanut butter, fennel and cumin seeds, ground coriander, pepper and chillies. Cook for 1 minute, then add the chicken, turning in the mixture until evenly coated.
4. Add the coconut liquid and lemon peel, bring to the boil, then cover and simmer for 35–40 minutes, until the chicken is tender. Stir in the lemon juice. Garnish with coriander leaves and serve with rice flavoured with herbs and poppadums.

KASHMIRI CHICKEN PILAU

500 g (1 lb) Basmati rice
4 tablespoons oil
2 onions, chopped
2 cloves garlic, crushed
2.5 cm (1 inch) piece fresh
   ginger root, peeled and
   chopped
2 teaspoons cumin seeds
750 g (1¹/₂ lb) boneless
   chicken breast, cubed
1 teaspoon saffron strands
300 ml (1¹/₄ cups) boiling
   water

6 cardamom pods, bruised
4 tablespoons chopped
   mint
1 teaspoon curry powder
2.5 cm (1 inch) piece
   cinnamon stick
125 g (4 oz) frozen peas
250 g (8 oz) tomatoes,
   skinned and chopped
125 ml (¹/₂ cup) raisins
salt to taste
125 ml (¹/₂ cup) blanched
   almonds, toasted, to
   garnish

1. Rinse the rice several times in cold water, then drain and leave to dry.

2. Heat half the oil in a large heavy-based pan, add half of the onion, the garlic, ginger and cumin seeds and fry for 5 minutes.

3. Add the chicken and cook, stirring, until browned all over. Add the saffron, water, cardamom pods, mint, curry powder and cinnamon stick. Bring to the boil, then cover and simmer for 25 minutes, until the chicken is tender. Transfer to a bowl and rinse out the pan.

4. Heat the remaining oil in the pan, add remaining onion and fry until lightly coloured. Stir in the rice and cook gently for 2–3 minutes, until it becomes opaque.

5. Add the chicken mixture, peas, tomatoes, raisins and salt. Stir gently, then shake the pan to level the ingredients. Add sufficient boiling water to come 2 cm (¾ inch) above the top of the rice. Cover the pan tightly and cook gently for 20–25 minutes, until the rice is tender and all the liquid is absorbed. Discard the cinnamon stick.

6. Transfer to a warmed serving dish and sprinkle with the almonds. Serve with mango chutney, poppadums, and chilled yogurt mixed with chopped cucumber.

Serves 6
Preparation time:
30 minutes
Cooking time:
1 hour
Freezing:
Not recommended

VEGETARIAN DISHES

PAPRIKA BEAN CASSEROLE

250 g (8 oz) dried white
   beans, soaked overnight
3 tablespoons oil
1 clove garlic, crushed
3 onions, sliced
2 green peppers, cored,
   seeded and sliced
2 tablespoons paprika

1 teaspoon liquid honey
2 × 398 ml (14 oz) cans
   tomatoes
2 tablespoons tomato paste
salt and pepper to taste
parsley sprigs to garnish

Serves 4
Preparation time:
30 minutes, plus
soaking time
Cooking time:
1 hour 40 minutes
Freezing:
Recommended

1. Drain and rinse the beans and place in a pan. Cover
with cold water, bring to the boil and boil for 10 minutes,
then cover and simmer for about 1 hour, until tender.
Drain well.
2. Heat the oil in a large pan, add the garlic and onion and
fry until softened and lightly browned. Add the peppers
and fry for 5 minutes.
3. Add the beans and remaining ingredients, bring to the
boil, then cover and simmer for 25 minutes.
4. Garnish with parsley to serve.

CASHEW NUT AND SESAME PILAF

2 tablespoons oil
2 tablespoons butter
1 onion, chopped
1 red pepper, cored, seeded
   and chopped
250 ml (1 cup) brown rice
25 g (1 oz) sesame seeds
5 tablespoons white wine

750 ml (3 cups) Rich
   Vegetable Stock*
2 teaspoons soy sauce
2 carrots, grated
2 zucchini, grated
125 g (4 oz) cashew nuts
4 green onions, chopped
salt and pepper to taste

Serves 4
Preparation time:
35 minutes
Cooking time:
45 minutes
Freezing:
Not recommended

1. Heat the oil and butter in a heavy-based pan, add the
onion and fry until softened. Add the red pepper, rice and
sesame seeds and stir well, until all the rice grains are
coated in oil.
2. Stir in the wine, stock and soy sauce and bring to the
boil, then cover and cook gently for 35 minutes, until
almost all of the liquid is absorbed.
3. Stir in the remaining ingredients, cover and cook for 10
minutes, until the rice is tender. Serve hot.

CHILLI BEAN POT

The pulses I have suggested here give a good colour combination and have similar cooking times.

250 g (8 oz) dried red
  kidney beans, soaked
  overnight
125 g (4 oz) each dried
  black-eyed beans and
  chick peas, soaked
  overnight
2 tablespoons oil
2 onions, chopped
1 clove garlic, crushed
1–2 teaspoons hot chilli
  powder

2 × 398 ml (14 oz) cans
  tomatoes
1/2 teaspoon caraway seeds
150 ml (2/3 cup) Rich
  Vegetable Stock*
1 green pepper, cored,
  seeded and chopped
125 g (4 oz) mushrooms,
  chopped
salt and pepper to taste
TO SERVE:
4 tablespoons yogurt
paprika

Serves 4–6
Preparation time:
20 minutes, plus
soaking time
Cooking time:
1½–1¾ hours
Freezing:
Recommended at
end of stage 3

1. Drain and rinse the beans and place in a large pan. Cover with cold water, bring to the boil and boil hard for 10 minutes, then partly cover and simmer for about 45 minutes, until almost tender. Drain well and rinse the pan.
2. Heat the oil in the pan, add the onion and garlic and cook until softened. Add the chilli powder, tomatoes, caraway seeds, stock and green pepper and bring to the boil. Add the beans and simmer for 25–30 minutes.
3. Stir in the mushrooms, and salt and pepper, and cook for 10–20 minutes, until the beans are tender.
4. Top each portion with a little yogurt and paprika.

VEGETABLE HOTPOT WITH STILTON CROÛTONS

1 small turnip, diced
1 parsnip, diced
350 g (12 oz) potatoes
  diced
4 celery sticks, chopped
4 leeks, sliced
3 tablespoons butter or
  margarine
50 ml (1/4 cup) flour
150 ml (2/3 cup) yogurt
50 g (2 oz) walnut halves
2 teaspoons Dijon mustard

2 tablespoons chopped
  parsley
salt and pepper to taste
celery leaves to garnish
FOR THE CROÛTONS:
75 g (3 oz) Stilton cheese,
  crumbled
2 tablespoons butter,
  softened
3 slices whole wheat bread,
  toasted
paprika

1. Place the turnip and parsnip in a saucepan with salted water to cover. Bring to the boil, then cover and simmer for 5 minutes. Add the potatoes and celery and cook for 10 minutes, then add the leeks and cook for about 5 minutes, until all the vegetables are tender. Strain, reserving the liquid, and set aside.

2. Melt the butter or margarine in the saucepan, add the flour and cook for 1 minute. Gradually add 300 ml (1¼ cups) of the reserved vegetable liquid, making up with water if necessary, and cook, stirring, until thickened and smooth. Add the yogurt, walnuts, mustard, and salt and pepper and simmer for 2 minutes. Stir in the vegetables and parsley and mix well. Transfer to a 1.75 litre (7 cup) ovenproof dish and spread evenly.

3. To make the croûtons, beat together the Stilton and butter until smooth. Spread thickly over the bread, then cut into small cubes, about 12 from each slice.

4. Arrange the bread, cheese side up, over the vegetables, to cover them completely. Sprinkle with paprika and bake in a preheated oven, 200°C/400°F, for 20 minutes, until the topping is crisp and golden. Garnish with celery leaves and serve with a mixed salad.

Serves 4
Preparation time:
45 minutes
Cooking time:
20 minutes
Freezing:
Not recommended

DHAL SAMBAR

Don't be put off by the inclusion of whole chillies in this recipe—it's not as hot as it may appear, as the lentils add a creamy taste to offset the fire!

250 g (8 oz) red lentils	*2 tablespoons oil*
600 ml (2½ cups) water	*2 onions, chopped*
1 teaspoon turmeric	*2 cloves garlic, crushed*
3 green chillies, halved	*1 cm (½ inch) piece fresh*
lengthways	*ginger root, peeled and*
1 tablespoon chopped	*chopped finely*
coriander leaves	*1 teaspoon cumin seeds*
250 g (8 oz) egg plant, cut	*½ teaspoon each*
into strips	*fenugreek and black*
248 ml (10 oz) can	*mustard seeds*
tomatoes	*½ teaspoon salt*

Serves 4
Preparation time:
20 minutes
Cooking time:
40 minutes
Freezing:
Recommended

1. Place the lentils and water in a saucepan, bring to the boil, then simmer for 10 minutes. Stir in the turmeric, chillies, coriander, egg plant and tomatoes with their juice. Bring to the boil, then cover and simmer for 30 minutes, until the lentils are soft and pulpy.
2. Meanwhile, heat the oil in a frying pan, add the onion and fry until softened and golden brown. Add the garlic, ginger, cumin, fenugreek and mustard seeds and fry for 2 minutes.
3. Add to the lentils with the salt and stir well. Serve with spiced Basmati rice and poppadums.

MEDITERRANEAN VEGETABLE STEW

Ratatouille is traditionally made with a lot of oil. This is a lighter version which uses just a little oil and stews the vegetables in tomato sauce.

350 g (12 oz) egg plant,	*6 basil leaves, chopped*
cut into large cubes	*roughly*
2 tablespoons olive oil	*1 teaspoon chopped*
1 Spanish onion, chopped	*oregano*
2 cloves garlic, crushed	*250 g (8 oz) zucchini,*
1 each red, yellow and	*sliced thickly*
green pepper, cored,	*175 g (6 oz) mushrooms*
seeded and cut into	*salt and pepper to taste*
2.5 cm (1 inch) cubes	*cheese bread to serve (see*
550 g (1.2 lb) jar passata	*right)*

1. Place the egg plant in a colander, sprinkle with salt, place a plate on top and leave to drain for 30 minutes. Rinse and dry with paper towels.

2. Heat the oil in a heavy-based saucepan, add the onion and garlic and fry until softened. Add the peppers and fry for 5 minutes.

3. Add the egg plant, passata, herbs, and salt and pepper, bring to the boil, then cover and simmer for 20 minutes.

4. Add the zucchini and mushrooms and cook for 25 minutes, until the vegetables are tender. Serve with hot cheese bread.

To make cheese bread: Cut a small French stick into thick slices, without cutting right through. Grate 50 g (2 oz) old Cheddar cheese and mix into 125 ml (½ cup) softened butter. Spread over the cut surfaces, wrap tightly in foil and bake in a preheated oven, 200°C/400°F, for about 15 minutes, until the butter has melted and the bread is crisp.

Serves 4
Preparation time:
45 minutes
Cooking time:
45 minutes
Freezing:
Recommended

EGG PLANT AND CHEESE BAKE

This is a very popular dish which can be assembled several hours in advance, ready to go in the oven.

2 egg plants, sliced
1 egg, beaten
150 ml (²⁄₃ cup) whole
*   wheat breadcrumbs*
6 tablespoons olive oil
398 ml (14 oz) can
*   tomatoes*
1 teaspoon chopped
*   oregano*
1 clove garlic, crushed

1 tablespoon tomato paste
1 teaspoon liquid honey
150 ml (²⁄₃ cup) red wine
175 g (6 oz) Mozzarella
*   cheese, sliced*
50 g (2 oz) Parmesan
*   cheese, grated*
salt and pepper to taste
garlic bread to serve (see
*   opposite)*

Serves 4
Preparation time:
30 minutes
Cooking time:
40–45 minutes
Freezing:
Not recommended

1. Coat the egg plant slices in the egg and breadcrumbs. Heat half of the oil in a large pan, add half of the egg plant slices and fry on both sides until lightly browned. Drain on paper towels. Repeat with the remaining egg plants and oil.

2. Place the tomatoes, oregano, garlic, tomato paste, honey, wine, and salt and pepper in a saucepan. Bring to the boil, stirring, then simmer for 5 minutes.

3. Arrange half of the egg plant slices in an oiled oven-proof dish and cover with half of the Mozzarella cheese. Repeat the layers. Pour over the tomato sauce and sprinkle with the Parmesan cheese.

4. Cook in a preheated oven, 190°C/375°F, for 40–45 minutes, until the egg plants are tender and the topping is golden brown. Serve with garlic bread.

MINESTRONE CASSEROLE WITH PESTO

2 tablespoons olive oil
1 large onion, sliced thinly
1 egg plant, diced
500 g (1 lb) tomatoes,
*   skinned and chopped*
75 g (3 oz) small pasta
*   shapes*
125 g (4 oz) cabbage,
*   shredded*
398 ml (14 oz) can red
*   kidney beans, drained*

125 g (4 oz) green beans,
*   cut into 2.5 cm (1 inch)*
*   lengths*
2 zucchini, sliced
150 ml (²⁄₃ cup) Rich
*   Vegetable Stock**
2 tablespoons pesto
salt and pepper to taste
TO SERVE:
25–50 g (1–2 oz)
*   Parmesan cheese, grated*
garlic bread (see right)

1. Heat the oil in a large pan, add the onion and fry until softened. Add the egg plant and tomatoes and cook gently for 10 minutes.

2. Meanwhile, cook the pasta shapes in boiling salted water for 5 minutes; drain well.

3. Add to the pan with the cabbage, beans, zucchini, stock, and salt and pepper. Bring back to the boil, then cover and simmer for 15–20 minutes, until the vegetables are tender.

4. Just before serving, add the pesto. Sprinkle each portion with Parmesan cheese, and serve with garlic bread.

Serves 4
Preparation time: 30 minutes
Cooking time: 25–30 minutes
Freezing: Recommended at end of stage 3

To make garlic bread: Cut a small French stick into thick slices, without cutting right through. Mix 125 ml (½ cup) softened butter with 3 crushed cloves garlic. Spread over the cut surfaces, wrap tightly in foil and bake in a pre-heated oven, 200°C/400°F, for about 15 minutes, until the butter has melted and the bread is crisp.

LEEK AND BROAD BEAN RAGOÛT

Although this is fine as a complete meal, for non-vegetarians it can also be served as a substantial accompaniment for broiled meats or sausages.

*50 ml (¹⁄4 cup) butter or
   margarine
750 g (1¹⁄2 lb) potatoes, cut
   into 1 cm (¹⁄2 inch) thick
   rounds
2 cloves garlic, crushed
50 ml (¹⁄4 cup) flour
300 ml (1¹⁄4 cups) Rich
   Vegetable Stock*
1 teaspoon chopped thyme*

*1 kg (2 lb) fresh broad
   beans, or 500 g (1 lb)
   frozen
2 leeks, sliced thickly
250 ml (1 cup) sour cream
2 tablespoons chopped
   parsley
salt and pepper to taste*

Serves 4
Preparation time:
30 minutes
Cooking time:
25–30 minutes
Freezing:
Recommended

1. Melt the butter or margarine in a large heavy-based pan, add the potatoes and fry until lightly coloured. Add the garlic and cook for 1 minute.
2. Add the flour and cook for 1 minute, stirring well. Gradually add the stock and cook, stirring, until thickened. Add the thyme, cover and cook for 10 minutes.
3. Add the beans, leeks, sour cream, and salt and pepper and stir well. Cover and cook for 15–20 minutes, until the vegetables are tender. Sprinkle with chopped parsley just before serving.

CAULIFLOWER BHAJI

Cauliflower is one of my favourite vegetables in curries as it seems to absorb the delicious sauce. Use the whole cauliflower—slice the stalk thinly and chop the leaves.

3 tablespoons oil
1 teaspoon cumin seeds
2 onions, sliced thinly
2 cloves garlic, crushed
1 large cauliflower, broken into florets
500 g (1 lb) potatoes, cubed
½ teaspoon ground coriander
1 teaspoon turmeric

1 red chilli, sliced thinly
150 ml (⅔ cup) water
150 ml (⅔ cup) yogurt
250 g (8 oz) frozen peas
1 tablespoon chopped coriander leaves
2 teaspoons garam masala
salt to taste
coriander leaves to garnish

1. Heat the oil in a large saucepan, add the cumin seeds, onions and garlic and fry until softened. Add the cauli-flower and potatoes and cook, stirring, for 5 minutes.

2. Sprinkle in the ground coriander, turmeric and chilli and mix well. Add the water and yogurt and bring to the boil, then partly cover and simmer for 10–15 minutes, until the vegetables are almost tender.

3. Add the remaining ingredients and cook for 5 minutes. Garnish with coriander leaves to serve.

Serves 4
Preparation time: 35 minutes
Cooking time: 20–25 minutes
Freezing: Not recommended

SPINACH AND ZUCCHINI TIAN

This is a deliciously light dish best made in the summer with tiny sweet zucchini and young spinach leaves.

2 tablespoons butter
1 tablespoon oil
1 clove garlic, crushed
750 g (1½ lb) zucchini, grated
500 g (1 lb) spinach, chopped roughly

2 eggs, beaten
250 ml (1 cup) table cream
25 g (1 oz) Parmesan cheese, grated finely
salt, pepper and nutmeg to taste

Serves 4
Preparation time:
30 minutes
Cooking time:
35–40 minutes
Freezing:
Not recommended

1. Heat the butter and oil in a pan, add the garlic and fry for 1 minute. Add the zucchini and spinach and stir to coat in the oil. Cover and cook gently for 5 minutes, until the spinach has wilted. Transfer to a buttered ovenproof dish.
2. Beat together the eggs, cream, and salt, pepper and nutmeg and add to the dish. Sprinkle with the cheese.
3. Place the dish on a baking sheet and cook in a preheated oven, 180°C/350°F, for 35–40 minutes, until the mixture has set lightly and the top is golden.
4. Serve with sesame bread and a tomato and basil salad.

BROWN RICE BIRYANI

Serve 1 or 2 Indian salads with this dish: try a mixture of yogurt, chopped cucumber and ground cumin, or chopped onion and tomato, sprinkled with lemon juice.

2 tablespoons oil
1 onion, chopped
1 cm (½ inch) piece fresh ginger root, peeled and chopped finely
1 clove garlic, crushed
½ teaspoon each cumin and fenugreek seeds
250 ml (1 cup) long-grain brown rice
600 ml (2½ cups) Rich Vegetable Stock*
2.5 cm (1 inch) piece cinnamon stick
4 cloves
2 bay leaves

5 cardamom pods, bruised
½ teaspoon turmeric
½ teaspoon salt
150 ml (⅔ cup) yogurt
125 g (4 oz) cashew nuts
125 ml (½ cup) raisins
1 teaspoon garam masala
50 g (2 oz) button mushrooms, sliced
TO SERVE:
2 hard-boiled eggs, chopped
25 g (1 oz) shelled pistachio nuts, skinned

1. Heat the oil in a large pan with a tightly fitting lid. Add the onion, ginger, garlic, and cumin and fenugreek seeds and fry until the onion is lightly browned.

2. Stir in the rice and cook, stirring, until coated in oil. Add the stock, cinnamon, cloves, bay leaves, cardamom pods and turmeric, bring to the boil, then add the salt. Cover and cook gently for 30 minutes, until all the liquid is absorbed; add a little more stock if the pan becomes too dry.

3. Stir in the yogurt, cashew nuts, raisins, garam masala and mushrooms, cover and cook gently for 15 minutes.

4. Turn the biryani into a warmed serving dish and sprinkle the egg and pistachio nuts over the top. Serve with poppadums and Indian salads (see left).

Serves 4
Preparation time:
25 minutes
Cooking time:
45 minutes
Freezing:
Not recommended

KITCHERI

Mung dhal are tiny split green lentils. If you are unable to buy them, use red lentils or split peas instead. This dish can be served on its own or with chopped tomatoes moistened with yogurt and sprinkled with paprika.

2 tablespoons oil
2.5 cm (1 inch) piece fresh ginger root, peeled and chopped finely
1 onion, chopped finely
1 teaspoon cumin seeds
½ teaspoon fenugreek seeds
500 g (1 lb) Basmati rice
125 g (4 oz) mung dhal
1 litre (4 cups) water
2 bay leaves
1 cinnamon stick
2 tablespoons chopped coriander leaves

1 teaspoon saffron strands
2 green chillies (optional), seeded and chopped finely
125 g (4 oz) green beans, cut into 2.5 cm (1 inch) lengths
2 carrots, chopped
175 g (6 oz) cauliflower (optional), broken into small florets
salt to taste

Serves 4
Preparation time: 25 minutes
Cooking time: 40 minutes
Freezing: Not recommended

1. Heat the oil in a large pan with a tightly fitting lid. Add the ginger, onion, and cumin and fenugreek seeds and fry gently until the onion is lightly browned.
2. Stir in the rice and dhal and cook, stirring, until well coated in oil. Add the water, bay leaves, cinnamon, chopped coriander, saffron, and chillies if using. Bring to the boil, then cover and simmer for 15 minutes, until the water is beginning to be absorbed.
3. Add the remaining ingredients, stir gently, then cover and cook gently for 25 minutes, or until the rice is cooked and the vegetables are just tender.

CHEESE, SPINACH AND POTATO LAYER

1 kg (2 lb) fresh spinach, or 500 g (1 lb) frozen leaf
2 tablespoons oil
175 g (6 oz) mushrooms, sliced
1 teaspoon chopped oregano
500 g (1 lb) potatoes, boiled and diced

250 ml (1 cup) dry curd cheese
2 eggs, beaten
75 g (3 oz) Cheddar cheese, grated
3 tablespoons grated Parmesan cheese
salt, pepper and nutmeg to taste

1. If using fresh spinach, place in a pan with just the water that clings to the leaves after washing, cover and cook for 5 minutes, until tender. Drain and chop. If using frozen spinach, heat gently in a covered pan until defrosted, then drain, pressing out as much liquid as possible.

2. Heat the oil in a pan, add the mushrooms and fry until softened. Mix with the spinach, oregano, and a little nutmeg, salt and pepper. Transfer to a buttered ovenproof dish and cover with the potatoes.

3. Beat together the remaining ingredients, season with salt and pepper, then spread over the potatoes.

4. Cook in a preheated oven, 180°C/350°F, for 40 minutes, until risen and deep golden brown. Serve immediately, with a mixed salad if you wish.

Serves 4
Preparation time:
30 minutes
Cooking time:
40 minutes
Freezing:
Not recommended

SWEET POTATO AND CELERIAC BAKE

500 g (1 lb) sweet potatoes
500 g (1 lb) celeriac,
  peeled
250 ml (1 cup) sour
  cream
125 g (4 oz) Gruyère
  cheese, grated
25 g (1 oz) Parmesan
  cheese, grated finely

1 small onion, chopped
  finely
3 green onions, chopped
  finely
50 ml (¼ cup) oatmeal
1 tablespoon butter
salt and pepper to taste

Serves 4
Preparation time:
30 minutes
Cooking time:
1 hour
Freezing:
Not recommended

1. Cut the potatoes and celeriac into thin slices; cut the slices into halves or quarters if large. Parboil in salted water for 5 minutes, then drain.
2. Mix together the sour cream, cheeses, onion, green onions, and salt and pepper.
3. Place half of the potatoes and celeriac in a buttered ovenproof dish. Spread with half of the cream mixture. Repeat the layers. Sprinkle with the oatmeal and dot with the butter.
4. Bake in a preheated oven, 180°C/350°F, for 1 hour, until the vegetables are tender and the topping is golden brown. Serve with a green salad if you wish.

WINTER NUT CRUMBLE

175 g (6 oz) carrots,
  chopped roughly
2 parsnips, diced
1 small turnip, diced
1 leek, sliced
150 ml (⅔ cup) milk
300 ml (1¼ cups) Rich
  Vegetable Stock*
398 ml (14 oz) can
  chestnuts, drained

2 tablespoons corn starch,
  blended with 1
  tablespoon water
salt and pepper to taste
fresh herbs to garnish
FOR THE TOPPING:
25 g (1 oz) sunflower seeds
25 g (1 oz) chopped nuts
125 ml (½ cup) whole
  wheat breadcrumbs
50 g (2 oz) Lancashire or
  Cheddar cheese, grated

Serves 4
Preparation time:
40 minutes
Cooking time:
About 30 minutes
Freezing:
Recommended

1. Place the vegetables in a pan with the milk and stock and bring to the boil. Partly cover and simmer for 15–20 minutes, until almost tender. Add the chestnuts, and salt and pepper, and stir well.
2. Stir in the blended corn starch and cook until thickened and smooth, stirring constantly.

3. Transfer the mixture to a warmed ovenproof dish. Mix together the topping ingredients and sprinkle evenly over the top. Place under a preheated broiler for 5 minutes, until the topping is crisp and golden brown. Serve immediately, garnished with fresh herbs.

MONGOLIAN HOTPOT

This dish is the Chinese version of a fondue—the morsels of food are cooked in simmering stock at the table, then dipped into various sauces. If you don't happen to have an authentic Chinese firepot, use a fondue pot, or a small electric ring with a flameproof casserole on top. The food is removed from the stock, using small wire baskets which are available from Chinese shops. Serve the hotpot with a bowl of boiled rice and jasmine tea.

1.75 kg (4 lb) lamb fillet
175 g (6 oz) rice vermicelli
or egg noodles
500 g (1 lb) pak choi or
spring greens, shredded
500 g (1 lb) Chinese
cabbage, shredded
250 g (8 oz) bean sprouts
1.75 litres (7 cups) Chicken
Stock*

green onion brushes (see
page 69) to garnish
FOR THE DIPS:
6 tablespoons soy sauce
1 tablespoon finely
chopped green onion
1 teaspoon grated fresh
ginger root
4 tablespoons chilli sauce
4 tablespoons hoisin sauce

Serves 8–10
Preparation time:
45 minutes
Cooking time:
Variable
(depending on
stock temperature,
number of diners,
etc)
Freezing:
Not recommended

1. Using a large very sharp knife, cut the lamb into very thin slices.
2. Break up the rice vermicelli, if using, and place in a large bowl. Cover with hot water and soak for 15 minutes, until softened; drain. If using egg noodles, cook according to packet instructions; drain.
3. Arrange the lamb, rice vermicelli or egg noodles, pak choi or spring greens, Chinese cabbage and bean sprouts on several serving dishes around the table. Garnish with green onion brushes. Bring the stock to the boil.
4. Mix together the soy sauce, green onion and ginger. Place in several tiny dishes. Put the chilli sauce and hoisin sauce into several more dishes. Place on the table.
5. Bring the boiling stock to the table. Each diner should have a dinner plate or Chinese bowl, a set of chopsticks and a wire basket. The basket is filled with morsels of food, then lowered into the stock until the food is cooked. The stock must be kept simmering.
6. Use the dips to accompany the food. The food imparts ever increasing flavour to the stock, which is finally drunk as a soup in small bowls at the end of the meal.

CHINESE BRAISED LAMB

This aromatic lamb dish is wonderful for a special occasion. It can be prepared up to the end of stage 2 the day before, if necessary.

2 tablespoons oil
750 g (1½ lb) boneless lamb, e.g. tenderloin or leg, cut into 3.5 cm (1½ inch) pieces
2 slices fresh ginger root, cut into thin strips
1 onion, sliced thinly
450 ml (1¾ cups) Chicken Stock*

75 ml (⅓ cup) light brown sugar
2 tablespoons soy sauce
2.5 cm (1 inch) piece cinnamon stick
1 tablespoon smooth peanut butter
1 tablespoon hoisin sauce
8 green onions
125 g (4 oz) mushrooms, sliced

Serves 4
Preparation time: 25 minutes
Cooking time: 1–1¼ hours
Freezing: Recommended at end of stage 2

1. Heat the oil in a large pan, add the lamb and fry quickly, stirring, until browned. Add the ginger and onion and fry until softened.
2. Add the stock, sugar, soy sauce, cinnamon, peanut butter and hoisin sauce, bring to the boil, stirring, then cover and simmer for 1–1¼ hours, until the lamb is tender.
3. Meanwhile, make brushes (see page 69) from 4 of the green onions; slice the remainder diagonally.
4. Five minutes before the end of the cooking time, add the sliced green onions and mushrooms to the lamb.
5. Serve garnished with the green onion brushes, and accompanied by boiled rice and blanched lettuce leaves sprinkled with oyster sauce.

PORK IN CIDER

Pork is generally a tender meat which needs less cooking than you might imagine.

50 ml (¼ cup) flour
2 teaspoons paprika
1 teaspoon mustard powder
750 g (1½ lb) lean pork, cut into cubes
2 tablespoons oil
1 onion, sliced

450 ml (1¾ cups) dry cider
1 cooking apple, peeled, cored and sliced
1 small red pepper, cored, seeded and diced
3 tablespoons whipping cream
salt and pepper to taste

1. Mix together the flour, paprika and mustard and use to coat the pork.
2. Heat the oil in a heavy-based saucepan, add the onion and fry until softened. Add the pork and fry until browned all over. Add any leftover flour mixture and cook for 1 minute.
3. Gradually stir in the cider and cook, stirring, until thickened and smooth. Add the apple, and salt and pepper and stir well. Cover and simmer for 40 minutes, until the pork is tender; add the red pepper after 25 minutes.
4. Just before serving, stir in the cream and heat through. Serve with pasta and a green salad.

Serves 4
Preparation time: 25 minutes
Cooking time: 40 minutes
Freezing: Recommended at end of stage 3

CASSOULET ROBERT

Cassoulet originates in South West France, where every town has its own version. This recipe may not be strictly authentic, but it is greatly enjoyed in our household.

500 g (1 lb) dried white beans, soaked overnight	*4 cloves garlic*
750 g (1½ lb) salt pork	*500 g (1 lb) ripe tomatoes, skinned and quartered*
half shoulder of lamb, weighing about 750 g (1½ lb), boned	*1 tablespoon oil*
4 leeks	*500 g (1 lb) coarse spicy sausage, preferably Toulouse*
4 large carrots	*125 ml (½ cup) fresh brown breadcrumbs*
2 cloves	*salt and pepper to taste*
1 large onion	*thyme sprigs to garnish*
2 thyme sprigs	

Serves 8
Preparation time:
30 minutes, plus soaking time
Cooking time:
4 hours
Freezing:
Recommended

1. Drain and rinse the beans and cook in boiling water for 10 minutes. Drain, then place in a very large pan with water to cover. Bury the pork and lamb in the beans.
2. Tie 2 leeks together. Halve 2 carrots lengthways. Stick the cloves into the onion. Place these vegetables in the pan with the thyme, 2 garlic cloves and plenty of black pepper.
3. Bring slowly to the boil, skimming off any scum that rises to the surface, then cover and simmer for about 1½ hours, skimming occasionally, until the beans are tender.
4. Remove the meat and strain the beans, reserving the stock. Remove the vegetables and thyme from the beans. Taste the stock and add salt if necessary.
5. Remove the rind from the pork. Cut the pork and lamb into 2.5 cm (1 inch) chunks.
6. Crush the remaining garlic and mix with the tomatoes.
7. Place half of the beans in a large casserole. Cover with the meat, then the tomatoes. Place the remaining beans on top. Pour over 600 ml (2½ cups) of the reserved stock and cover tightly.
8. Cook in a preheated oven, 140°C/275°F, for 1½ hours; add more stock if it becomes too dry.
9. Heat the oil in a pan, add the sausage and fry until well browned. Drain and cut into 5 cm (2 inch) lengths. Stir into the beans. Sprinkle the breadcrumbs over the top. Return to the oven, uncovered, for 1 hour, until the top is crusty and golden brown.
10. Serve garnished with thyme, with plenty of warm French bread to mop up the juices, and a green salad.

BRAISED STUFFED PORK TENDERLOIN

1 pork tenderloin, weighing about 500 g (1 lb)	*300 ml (1¼ cups) Light Meat Stock**
50 g (2 oz) dried apricots, soaked if necessary	*2 tablespoons lemon juice*
4–6 sage leaves	*125 g (4 oz) button mushrooms, sliced*
2 tablespoons roughly chopped parsley	*2 tablespoons sherry*
1 tablespoon oil	*150 ml (²/3 cup) sour cream*
1 onion, chopped finely	*salt and pepper to taste*
	sage leaves to garnish

Serves 4
Preparation time:
30 minutes
Cooking time:
35 minutes
Freezing:
Not recommended

1. Slice the pork tenderloin almost in half horizontally. Open out and flatten with a rolling pin or meat mallet. Arrange the apricots and sage leaves down one half and sprinkle with the parsley, and salt and pepper. Fold the other half over the filling and secure with cocktail sticks or fine string.

2. Heat the oil in a large frying pan with a lid, add the pork and fry until browned all over. Remove from the pan and keep warm.

3. Add the onion to the pan and fry until softened. Add the stock and lemon juice and bring to the boil. Return the meat to the pan, cover and simmer for 20 minutes.

4. Stir in the mushrooms and sherry and mix well. Season with salt and pepper. Cook for 15 minutes. Remove the pork, discarding the cocktail sticks or string, and keep warm.

5. Gradually stir the sour cream into the sauce, heating gently but not allowing it to boil.

6. Slice the pork thinly and arrange on warmed individual plates. Spoon the mushroom sauce around the pork and garnish with sage leaves. Serve with boiled new potatoes or plain boiled rice.

AFELIA

This is a typical Greek dish, using a few simple ingredients to maximum effect.

2 tablespoons coriander seeds	*2 tablespoons oil*
750 g (1½ lb) lean boneless pork, cubed	*1 onion, sliced thinly*
300 ml (1¼ cups) red wine	*2 teaspoons flour*
	salt and pepper to taste

1. Crush the coriander seeds lightly in a pestle and mortar or with the back of a wooden spoon. Place the pork in a china bowl. Add the coriander and wine, cover and marinate for at least 6 hours, or overnight if possible.

2. Remove the meat with a slotted spoon and dry with paper towels; reserve the marinade.

3. Heat the oil in a heavy-based pan, add the onion and fry until softened. Add the pork and fry until browned all over. Sprinkle in the flour and cook for 1 minute.

4. Gradually add the marinade, stirring until slightly thickened. Season with salt and pepper. Cover and simmer for 40–50 minutes, until the pork is tender.

5. Serve with tomato rice pilaf: cook the rice with 1 tablespoon tomato paste, then stir in a can of drained and halved artichoke hearts and chopped parsley to taste.

Serves 4
Preparation time: 25 minutes, plus marinating
Cooking time: 40–50 minutes
Freezing: Recommended

BEEF AND ROSEMARY ROLL-UPS

8 slices beef tenderloin
8 slices Parma ham
2 tablespoons chopped
*   parsley*
2 teaspoons finely chopped
*   rosemary*
25 g (1 oz) Parmesan
*   cheese, grated*
2 tablespoons oil

1 onion, chopped
150 ml (²/₃ cup) red wine
150 ml (²/₃ cup) Rich Beef
*   Stock**
250 g (8 oz) tomatoes,
*   skinned and chopped*
salt and pepper to taste
rosemary sprigs to garnish

Serves 4
Preparation time:
25 minutes
Cooking time:
50–60 minutes
Freezing:
Recommended

1. Sprinkle the beef slices with salt and pepper and place a slice of Parma ham on top. Mix together the parsley, rosemary and Parmesan. Place a little of the mixture on one end of each beef slice. Roll up, tucking in the ends to enclose the filling, and secure with fine string or cocktail sticks.
2. Heat the oil in a large saucepan, add the onion and fry until softened. Add the beef and fry until browned.
3. Add the wine, stock and tomatoes, bring to the boil, then cover and simmer for 50–60 minutes, until the beef is tender. Remove the string or cocktail sticks and arrange the beef on a warmed serving dish.
4. Pour over the sauce, garnish with rosemary and serve with rice cooked with chopped spinach and 1 tablespoon tomato paste.

BEEF IN RED WINE

An ideal dish for entertaining: it can be made up to two
    days in advance and, in fact, improves with reheating.

750 g (1½ lb) chuck steak
*   or top rump, cut into*
*   large cubes*
1 onion, sliced thinly
6 peppercorns
bouquet garni
2 tablespoons brandy
450 ml (1¾ cups) full
*   bodied red wine*
4 bacon slices, halved
2 tablespoons oil

2 tablespoons butter
250 g (8 oz) pickling
*   onions*
50 ml (¼ cup) flour
1 clove garlic, crushed
350 g (12 oz) button
*   mushrooms*
salt and pepper to taste
French bread slices,
*   toasted, to garnish*

1. Place the meat in a large bowl. Sprinkle with the onion

slices, then add the peppercorns, bouquet garni, brandy and wine. Stir well and leave to marinate for 3–4 hours, or overnight, stirring occasionally. Strain, reserving the marinade, and dry the meat with paper towels.

2. Stretch the bacon with the back of a knife, then roll up, securing with a cocktail stick if necessary.

3. Heat the oil and butter in a large pan, add the bacon rolls and fry until lightly browned. Remove with a slotted spoon and set aside.

4. Add the pickling onions to the pan and fry until lightly browned; remove and set aside.

5. Add the beef to the pan and fry over a high heat until evenly browned. Sprinkle in the flour and cook, stirring, for 1 minute. Add the reserved marinade and bring to the boil, stirring. Add the garlic, and salt and pepper, then cover and simmer for 2 hours, until tender.

6. Remove the cocktail sticks from the bacon rolls, add to the pan with the onions and mushrooms and simmer for 30 minutes. Garnish with toasted French bread to serve.

Serves 4
Preparation time:
30 minutes, plus
marinating
Cooking time:
2½ hours
Freezing:
Recommended

OSSO BUCCO WITH GREMOLATA

1 tablespoon flour
4 slices shank of veal,
  about 3.5 cm (1½
  inches) thick
2 tablespoons butter
1 tablespoon olive oil
2 onions, chopped
2 carrots, chopped
1 stick celery, chopped
300 ml (1¼ cups) dry
  white wine

248 ml (10 oz) can
  tomatoes
bouquet garni
2 strips lemon peel
salt and pepper to taste
FOR THE GREMOLATA:
1 teaspoon grated lemon
  peel
1 clove garlic, crushed
2 tablespoons chopped
  parsley

Serves 4
Preparation time:
30 minutes
Cooking time:
1 hour
Freezing:
Recommended

1. Season the flour with salt and pepper and use to coat the veal.
2. Heat the butter and oil in a slarge saucepan, add the veal and brown all over. Remove from the pan and set aside.
3. Add the onion, carrot and celery to the pan and fry for 5 minutes, until slightly softened. Add the remaining ingredients and bring to the boil. Return the veal to the pan, cover and simmer for 1 hour, until the veal is tender.
4. Mix together the gremolata ingredients. Sprinkle a little over each portion of osso bucco to serve.

BEEF IN WATERCRESS SAUCE

125 g (4 oz) zucchini,
  chopped finely
2 bacon slices, chopped
2 teaspoons capers,
  chopped
1 teaspoon chopped
  marjoram
1 teaspoon Dijon mustard
8 slices beef tenderloin
1 tablespoon oil
2 tablespoons butter
1 leek, chopped finely

150 ml (⅔ cup) dry white
  wine
1 bunch watercress
3 tablespoons whipping
  cream
salt and pepper to taste
TO GARNISH:
watercress sprigs
orange slices

1. Mix together the zucchini, bacon, capers, marjoram and mustard. Season lightly with salt and pepper. Lay the beef slices on a board. Place a little of the mixture on one end of each beef slice, roll up, tucking in the ends to enclose the zucchini filling, and secure with fine string or cocktail sticks.

2. Heat the oil and butter in a wide pan, add the beef and fry until lightly browned all over. Remove from the pan and set aside.

3. Add the leek to the pan and fry gently for 2 minutes. Stir in the wine and bring to the boil. Season with salt and pepper.

4. Return the beef to the pan, cover and simmer for 1 hour, until tender. Remove from the pan, remove the string or cocktail sticks and keep warm.

5. Add the watercress to the pan and cook for 1–2 minutes, until wilted but still bright green. Purée in a blender or food processor, return to the pan, stir in the cream and reheat gently.

6. Spoon a pool of sauce onto each warmed dinner plate and arrange 2 beef roll-ups on top. Garnish with watercress and orange and serve with tiny new potatoes.

Serves 4
Preparation time:
35 minutes
Cooking time:
1 hour
Freezing:
Not recommended

MONKFISH AND BACON WITH WINE AND HERB SAUCE

175 g (6 oz) side bacon slices, halved
750 g (1½ lb) monkfish, cut into 5 × 2.5 cm (2 × 1 inch) pieces
1 tablespoon olive oil
2 shallots, chopped
1 clove garlic, crushed
250 g (8 oz) small button mushrooms (optional)
1 teaspoon chopped dill

150 ml (⅔ cup) dry white wine
150 ml (⅔ cup) Chicken Stock*
2 teaspoons flour
2 tablespoons butter
4 tablespoons chopped parsley
salt and pepper to taste
dill sprigs to garnish

Serves 4
Preparation time:
30 minutes
Cooking time:
25–30 minutes
Freezing:
Not recommended

1. Stretch the bacon with the back of a knife and wrap a half slice around each piece of fish.
2. Heat the oil in a saucepan, add the fish and fry gently for about 5 minutes, until the bacon is lightly browned. Remove with a slotted spoon and set aside.
3. Add the shallots and garlic to the pan and fry until softened. Add the mushrooms, if using, and dill and cook, stirring, for 2 minutes. Add the wine and stock and bring to the boil.
4. Return the fish to the pan and simmer for 15–20 minutes, until tender. Season with salt and pepper.
5. Mash together the flour and butter until smooth. Add a little piece at a time to the simmering liquid, cooking until slightly thickened. Stir in the parsley. Serve garnished with dill, with a risotto of chopped tomatoes and peppers.

BLANQUETTE OF SOLE WITH CUCUMBER

Cooked cucumber may be unfamiliar to you, but it adds a fresh taste to the subtle fish and cream sauce.

8 lemon sole fillets, each weighing about 125 g (4 oz), skinned
½ cucumber, peeled
2 tablespoons butter
1 small onion, chopped finely

150 ml (⅔ cup) dry white wine
2 tablespoons freshly squeezed orange juice
150 ml (⅔ cup) table cream
1 egg yolk
salt and pepper to taste

1. Season the sole fillets on the skinned side with salt and pepper, then fold each into three.
2. Cut the cucumber into 2.5 cm (1 inch) slices, then cut each slice into quarters.
3. Melt the butter in a large frying pan with a lid. Add the onion and fry gently until softened. Add the cucumber and fry for 2 minutes.
4. Place the fish in the pan, pour over the wine and orange juice, bring to simmering point, then cover and cook for 7–10 minutes, until tender.
5. Transfer the fish and cucumber to a warmed serving dish with a fish slice, cover and keep warm while making the sauce.
6. Strain the pan juices, return to the pan and bring to the boil. Mix together the cream and egg yolk, stir into the pan and simmer gently, stirring constantly, until thickened. Check the seasoning.
7. Pour a little sauce over each fillet and hand the rest separately. Serve with new potatoes and a chicory and orange salad.

Serves 4
Preparation time:
30 minutes
Cooking time:
About 20 minutes
Freezing:
Not recommended

SAFFRON SEAFOOD CASSEROLE

50 ml (¼ cup) butter
1 clove garlic, crushed
2 onions, chopped
1 leek, sliced thinly
500 g (1 lb) haddock fillet, skinned and cubed
500 g (1 lb) small new potatoes
300 ml (1¼ cups) white wine
250 ml (1 cup) table cream

½ teaspoon saffron strands
125 g (4 oz) queen scallops
125 g (4 oz) shelled mussels
125 g (4 oz) peeled shrimps
125 g (4 oz) crabmeat
1 teaspoon chopped tarragon
salt and pepper to taste
tarragon sprigs to garnish

Serves 4
Preparation time:
25 minutes
Cooking time:
30–35 minutes
Freezing:
Not recommended

1. Melt the butter in a large pan, add the garlic, onion and leek and cook until softened. Add the haddock and potatoes and stir well.
2. Add the wine, cream and saffron, bring to the boil, then cover and simmer for 20 minutes.
3. Stir in the remaining ingredients carefully and simmer for 10–15 minutes, until the potatoes are tender.
4. Serve garnished with tarragon, with French bread.

CHICKEN RICE

This recipe is adapted from a Malaysian dish. The chicken is steamed over the aromatic rice to make it moist and tender. I serve a fiery dipping sauce with it.

500 g (1 lb) boneless chicken breast, cut into 2.5 cm (1 inch) cubes
2 tablespoons soy sauce
2 tablespoons oil
1 tablespoon grated fresh ginger root
2 cloves garlic, crushed
350 g (12 oz) Basmati rice
600 ml (2½ cups) Chicken Stock*

FOR THE DIPPING SAUCE:
1 red or green chilli
2 tablespoons grated fresh ginger root
2 cloves garlic, crushed
2 tablespoons sesame oil
salt to taste
TO GARNISH:
green onion brushes and chilli flowers (see right)
cucumber slices

1. Place the chicken and soy sauce in a bowl and mix well.
2. Heat the oil in a flameproof casserole, add the ginger and garlic and fry until lightly browned. Add the rice, stirring until coated in the oil.

3. Add the stock and a little salt, bring to the boil, then cover and simmer for about 5 minutes, until the rice has absorbed some of the stock.

4. Place the chicken over the rice in one layer and sprinkle with any remaining soy sauce. Cover and cook for 20–25 minutes, until the chicken and rice are tender.

5. Meanwhile, make the dipping sauce. Cut the chilli in half lengthways and remove the seeds and stalk. Chop the chilli very finely and mix in a small bowl with the ginger, garlic, sesame oil and a little salt.

6. Transfer the chicken rice to a warmed serving dish. Garnish with green onion brushes, chilli flowers and cucumber slices. Hand the dipping sauce separately.

To make green onion brushes: Cut the green onions into 5 cm (2 inch) lengths. Make cross-cuts at each end of each piece, almost to the centre. Place in iced, salted water to open out.

To make chilli flowers: Cut down the chilli from near the base to the tip. Make a second cut at right angles to this. Remove the seeds. Place in iced water and the chilli will open like a flower.

Serves 4
Preparation time:
25 minutes
Cooking time:
About 30 minutes
Freezing:
Not recommended

Illustrated on
page 71

HOWTOWDIE WITH DRAPPIT EGGS

Chicken has much more flavour cooked in a covered pot than when roasted—the flavours of the vegetables and seasonings really permeate the meat.

*1 chicken, with giblets,
    weighing 1.75 kb (4 lb)
125 ml (½ cup) fresh
    breadcrumbs
4 tablespoons milk
1 small onion, chopped
2 teaspoons chopped
    tarragon
1 tablespoon chopped
    parsley
50 ml (¼ cup) butter*

*8 shallots
2 celery sticks, chopped
pinch of ground mace
pinch of ground cloves
450 ml (1¾ cups) Chicken
    Stock*
4–6 eggs
150 ml (⅔ cup) whipping
    cream
750 g (1½ lb) spinach
salt and pepper to taste*

Serves 4–6
Preparation time:
40 minutes
Cooking time:
About 1¼ hours
Freezing:
Not recommended

Illustrated below
right: Chicken Rice
(page 68)

1. Remove the giblets from the chicken, rinse thoroughly and set aside. Wipe the chicken and sprinkle inside and out with salt and pepper.
2. Soak the breadcrumbs in the milk for a few minutes, until softened, then mix with the onion, herbs, and salt and pepper. Use to stuff the neck end of the chicken and secure with a fine skewer.
3. Melt the butter in a flameproof casserole, add the shallots and fry until lightly browned. Remove with a slotted spoon and set aside.
4. Add the chicken to the pan and fry until browned all over. Add the shallots, celery, mace, cloves, giblets and stock, bring to the boil, then cover tightly and cook for about 1¼ hours, until the chicken is tender.
5. Transfer the chicken to a serving dish and keep warm.
6. Strain the stock into a clean pan, pressing through as much of the chicken liver as possible; skim off any surface fat. Boil for 5 minutes, until reduced slightly, then lower the heat to simmer. Drop in the eggs and poach for 4–5 minutes, until set. Remove with a slotted spoon and keep warm in a shallow pan of warm water.
7. Meanwhile, cook the spinach in a covered pan, with no extra water, for about 5 minutes, until tender. Season with salt and pepper.
8. Stir the cream into the stock and reheat. Check the seasoning.
9. Arrange the spinach around the chicken and place the eggs on top. Pour a little sauce over the chicken and serve the remainder separately.

BRAISED CHICKEN BREASTS

1/2 teaspoon dried rosemary	*3 carrots*
1 clove garlic, crushed	*3 celery sticks*
2 tablespoons butter, softened	*2 leeks*
2 tablespoons grated Parmesan cheese	*1 tablespoon oil*
4 partly boned chicken breasts, each weighing about 175 g (6 oz)	*2 tablespoons butter*
	150 ml (2/3 cup) Chicken Stock*
	2 tablespoons lemon juice
	salt and pepper to taste

Serves 4
Preparation time:
35 minutes, plus
chilling
Cooking time:
30–35 minutes
Freezing:
Recommended

1. Mix together the rosemary, garlic, butter, cheese, and salt and pepper. Loosen the skin from the chicken and spread a little mixture between the flesh and skin. Smooth the skin back over the stuffing. Chill for 30 minutes.
2. Cut the carrots, celery and leeks into matchstick pieces.
3. Heat the oil and butter in a large heavy-based casserole, add the chicken and fry quickly until lightly browned. Remove from the pan.
4. Add the vegetables to the pan and fry for 5 minutes, until slightly softened. Add the stock, lemon juice, and a little salt and pepper. Bring to the boil.
5. Place the chicken breasts skin side up on top of the vegetables, cover and cook gently for 30–35 minutes, until tender. Accompany with a green salad and French bread.

BRAISED DUCK

Duck and orange are a classic combination.

1 duck breast joint, weighing 1 kg (2 lb)	*3 tablespoons freshly squeezed orange juice*
1 tablespoon oil	*4 tablespoons thick yogurt*
1 onion, chopped	*1 teaspoon corn starch*
2 carrots, chopped	*salt and pepper to taste*
150 ml (2/3 cup) white wine	*orange slices and chervil sprigs to garnish*
1/2 teaspoon grated orange peel	

1. Trim off any excess fat from the underside of the duck breast. Heat the oil in a flameproof casserole, add the duck, skin side down, and fry until well browned. Turn and fry the other side. Remove the duck and drain on paper towels.

2. Add the onion and carrot to the pan and fry until slightly softened. Add the wine and stir well, scraping up any sediment from the base of the pan. Add the orange peel, juice, and salt and pepper and bring to the boil.
3. Return the duck to the pan, cover and cook gently for 45 minutes, until tender. Remove the duck and keep warm.
4. Skim off any excess fat from the sauce, then purée in a blender or food processor and return to the pan.
5. Blend the yogurt with the corn starch, stir into the pan and cook until thickened. Check the seasoning.
6. Carefully remove the duck meat from the bone and slice thinly. Spoon a pool of sauce over each warm plate and arrange the duck on top. Garnish with halved orange slices and chervil and serve with tiny new potatoes and green beans or snow peas.

Serves 4
Preparation time:
30 minutes
Cooking time:
45 minutes
Freezing:
Not recommended

FRUITED GAME CASSEROLE

Choose plump birds for this casserole. The pheasant need not be the most young and tender specimen as the long slow cooking will tenderize an older bird.

2 tablespoons oil
1 oven-ready pheasant
2 pigeons
2 onions, chopped
2 carrots, chopped
3 celery sticks, chopped
450 ml (1¾ cups) red wine

150 ml (⅔ cup) water
2 bay leaves
2 tablespoons butter, softened
50 ml (¼ cup) flour
4 tablespoons ruby port
125 ml (½ cup) raisins
salt and pepper to taste

Serves 4
Preparation time: 40 minutes
Cooking time: 1¾–2¼ hours
Freezing: Recommended

1. Heat the oil in a flameproof casserole, add the pheasant and pigeons and fry until browned all over. Drain off any excess oil, then add the onion, carrot, celery, wine, water, bay leaves, and salt and pepper. Bring to the boil, cover and simmer for 1½–2 hours, until the meat is tender.
2. Lift out the birds and strip the meat from the bones. Chop into large pieces and return to the pan.
3. Place the butter and flour in a small bowl and work together with a teaspoon until well mixed. Add the paste, in small pieces, to the liquid and simmer, stirring, until thickened and smooth.
4. Add the port and raisins and simmer for 15 minutes. Check the seasoning and remove the bay leaves. Serve from the dish, accompanied by broccoli and cauliflower florets and sauté potatoes.

TURKEY FILLETS WITH ASPARAGUS AND PERNOD SAUCE

250 g (8 oz) asparagus
2 teaspoons flour
4 turkey fillets, each weighing about 125 g (4 oz)
2 tablespoons butter
2 shallots, chopped

300 ml (1¼ cups) Chicken Stock*
1 small potato, chopped finely
1 tablespoon Pernod
salt and pepper to taste

1. Remove the asparagus tips and set aside. Peel the stalks and slice thinly.
2. Season the flour with salt and pepper and use to coat the turkey fillets.

3. Heat the butter in a large frying pan with a lid. Add the turkey fillets and fry quickly on both sides until browned. Remove from the pan.

4. Add the shallots to the pan and fry until softened. Add the asparagus stalks and fry for 2 minutes. Add the stock, potato, Pernod, and salt and pepper and bring to the boil.

5. Return the turkey fillets to the pan, cover and simmer for 10–12 minutes, until the potato and asparagus are cooked and the turkey is tender.

6. Meanwhile, cook the asparagus tips in lightly salted water for 5–6 minutes, until just tender; drain.

7. Transfer the turkey fillets to warmed serving plates with a slotted spoon. Purée the sauce in a blender or food processor and pour around the turkey. Garnish with the asparagus tips and serve with a green salad.

Serves 4
Preparation time:
20 minutes
Cooking time:
About 15 minutes
Freezing:
Not recommended

HAM WITH LEEKS AND CELERIAC

50 g (2 oz) dried apricots, chopped	*1 small head celeriac, cut into sticks*
50 ml (¹/₄ cup) fresh brown breadcrumbs	*150 ml (²/₃ cup) Rich Vegetable Stock**
1 onion, chopped finely	*salt and pepper to taste*
1 tablespoon chopped parsley	*FOR THE SAUCE:*
2 tablespoons butter, melted	*150 ml (²/₃ cup) red wine*
4 thin ham steaks	*2 tablespoons redcurrant jelly*
2 leeks, cut into strips	*grated peel and juice of 1 orange and 1 lemon*
	1 teaspoon Dijon mustard

Serves 4
Preparation time:
35 minutes
Cooking time:
35 minutes
Freezing:
Recommended

1. Mix together the apricots, breadcrumbs, onion, parsley and butter. Season lightly with salt and pepper.
2. Divide the mixture between the ham steaks and roll up. Secure with fine string or cocktail sticks.
3. Place the leeks and celeriac in an ovenproof dish, arrange the ham roll-ups on top and add the stock. Cover and cook in a preheated oven, 180°C/350°F, for 35 minutes, until the ham and vegetables are tender.
4. Place all the sauce ingredients in a small pan and bring to the boil, stirring, then simmer for 5 minutes.
5. Arrange the vegetables and ham roll-ups on a warmed serving dish and serve with the sauce and zucchini.

VENISON AND REDCURRANT CASSEROLE

1 kg (2 lb) casserole venison, cut into 2.5 cm (1 inch) cubes	*2 onions*
	250 g (8 oz) side bacon slices, halved
450 ml (1³/₄ cups) red wine	*1 tablespoon flour*
	150 ml (²/₃ cup) Rich Beef Stock*
2 cloves garlic, bruised	
2 strips lemon peel	*125 g (4 oz) redcurrants*
2 tablespoons lemon juice	*4 tablespoons redcurrant jelly*
3 tablespoons olive oil	
1 cinnamon stick	*salt and pepper to taste*

1. Place the venison in a bowl and pour over the wine. Add the garlic, lemon peel and juice, 2 tablespoons of the oil and the cinnamon stick. Cover and leave to marinate in the refrigerator overnight.

2. Remove the venison with a slotted spoon and dry on paper towels; strain and reserve the marinade.

3. Cut each onion into 6 wedges. Stretch the bacon with the back of a knife, then roll up each piece.

4. Heat the remaining oil in a flameproof casserole, add the onion, fry until lightly browned, then remove.

5. Add the bacon rolls to the casserole and fry gently until the fat runs and they are lightly coloured. Remove with a slotted spoon.

6. Add the venison to the pan and fry until browned all over. Sprinkle in the flour and cook for 1 minute. Gradually stir in the reserved marinade and the stock and bring to the boil. Return the onions and bacon to the pan and stir well. Season with pepper, then cover and simmer for 2 hours, until the venison is tender.

7. Add the redcurrants and jelly to the pan and simmer for 10 minutes, until the redcurrants are tender and the jelly dissolved. Taste and add salt if necessary.

8. Serve with braised fennel and baked potatoes, topped with sour cream and chives.

Serves 4–6
Preparation time: 30 minutes, plus marinating
Cooking time: 2¼ hours
Freezing: Recommended

BASIC STOCK RECIPES

CHICKEN STOCK

1 kg (2 lb) chicken thighs,
   wings, drumsticks, or a
   mixture of these
1 onion
2 cloves
bouquet garni

celery leaves
2 slices fresh ginger root
10 black peppercorns
$1/2$ teaspoon salt
1.75 litres (7 cups) water

**Makes 1.5–1.75
litres (6–7 cups)**
Preparation time:
15 minutes, plus
cooling
Cooking time:
2 hours
Freezing:
Recommended

1. Cut up the chicken into small pieces and place in a large saucepan. Stick the onion with the cloves and add to the pan with the bouquet garni, celery leaves, ginger, peppercorns and salt.
2. Add the water and bring slowly to simmering point, skimming off any scum as it rises to the surface with a slotted spoon. Simmer the stock very gently, uncovered, for 2 hours, skimming occasionally.
3. Strain through a fine sieve into a large bowl and leave until cold. Remove any fat from the surface. Freeze in usable amounts.

RICH VEGETABLE STOCK

This concentrated stock is ideal as a base for casseroles, or can be served as a soup just as it is. Dilute it to make a lighter stock for sauces, etc.

2 carrots, chopped
3 potatoes, chopped
2 onions, chopped
25 g (1 oz) mushroom
   stalks
2 celery sticks, chopped

bouquet garni
2 bay leaves
8 black peppercorns
1 ripe tomato, chopped
1.75 litres (7 cups) water
salt to taste

**Makes about 1.75
litres (7 cups)**
Preparation time:
20 minutes, plus
cooling
Cooking time:
$1/2$–2 hours
Freezing:
Recommended

1. Place all the ingredients in a large saucepan and bring to the boil. Simmer very gently, uncovered, for 1½–2 hours, until the vegetables are very tender.
2. Strain through a sieve into a large bowl in batches, pressing through as many of the vegetables as possible. Leave until cold, then freeze in usable amounts.

LIGHT MEAT STOCK

This is a basic stock for using up leftover bones from a joint, chicken or turkey carcass, or uncooked bones from boned-out joints. Giblets can also be added for extra flavour.

1 kg (2 lb) meat bones or carcass, cooked or uncooked
1.75 litres (7 cups) water
2 onions, chopped

2 celery sticks, chopped
2 carrots, chopped
6 black peppercorns
bouquet garni
salt to taste

1. Place the bones or carcass in a large saucepan and cover with the water. Bring slowly to a gentle boil, skimming off any scum as it rises to the surface with a slotted spoon.
2. Add the remaining ingredients, partly cover and simmer for 3–4 hours, until clear.
3. Strain through a fine sieve into a large bowl and leave until cold. Remove any fat from the surface. Freeze in usable amounts.

Makes about 1.5 litres (6 cups)
Preparation time: 15 minutes, plus cooling
Cooking time: 3–4 hours
Freezing: Recommended

RICH BEEF STOCK

Use this stock for rich beef casseroles to give depth of flavour and a good rich colour.

500 g (1 lb) knuckle of veal, chopped
500 g (1 lb) shank of beef, chopped
1.75 litres (7 cups) water
1 onion, unpeeled, quartered

1 carrot, chopped
1 celery stick, chopped
bouquet garni
6 black peppercorns
salt to taste

1. Place the bones and beef in a large saucepan and cover with the water. Bring slowly to the boil, skimming off any scum as it rises to the surface with a slotted spoon. Simmer for 30 minutes, skimming occasionally.
2. Add the remaining ingredients, partly cover and simmer for 3 hours; do not allow the liquid to boil hard as this will make it cloudy.
3. Strain through a fine sieve into a large bowl and leave until cold. Remove any fat from the surface. Freeze in usable amounts.

Makes about 1.5 litres (6 cups)
Preparation time: 20 minutes, plus cooling
Cooking time: 3½ hours
Freezing: Recommended

INDEX

Photography by: Sara Taylor
Designed by: Sue Storey
Home economist: Mary Cadogan
Stylist: Tessa Rosier
Jacket photograph by: Clive Streeter
Illustration by: Linda Smith
Typeset by Rowland Phototypesetting Limited